W0036457

PENGUIN BUSINESS
THE INDIAN STOCK MARKET SIMPLIFIED

Pankaj Ladha, BCom, is an experienced financial expert with a strong background in commerce. Over the years, he has dedicated himself to helping retail investors understand and navigate the stock market effectively. With his practical insights and straightforward approach, Pankaj has simplified complex market concepts for investors, enabling them to make informed decisions and achieve financial success. His commitment to empowering individuals has made him a trusted mentor for numerous stock market enthusiasts.

Anant Ladha is a distinguished financial educator and professional with multiple qualifications, including CFA, CA, CFP, LLB and BCom. Known for his innovative and accessible approach to investing, he excels in breaking down intricate financial concepts into actionable strategies. With his deep expertise and extensive research, Anant has guided numerous investors towards unlocking opportunities in the stock market. His passion for financial education has established him as a leading authority in the field.

THE
INDIAN STOCK MARKET
SIMPLIFIED

A Beginner's Guide to Investing and Trading

PANKAJ LADHA
ANANT LADHA

PENGUIN
BUSINESS

An imprint of Penguin Random House

PENGUIN BUSINESS

Penguin Business is an imprint of the Penguin Random House group of companies
whose addresses can be found at global.penguinrandomhouse.com

Published by Penguin Random House India Pvt. Ltd
4th Floor, Capital Tower 1, MG Road,
Gurugram 122 002, Haryana, India

First published in Penguin Business by Penguin Random House India 2025

Copyright © Pankaj Ladha and Anant Ladha 2025

All rights reserved

10 9 8 7 6 5 4 3

The views and opinions expressed in this book are the authors' own and the
facts are as reported by them which have been verified to the extent possible,
and the publishers are not in any way liable for the same.

Please note that no part of this book may be used or reproduced in any manner
for the purpose of training artificial intelligence technologies or systems.

ISBN 9780143473039

Typeset in Adobe Caslon Pro by MAP Systems, Bengaluru, India
Printed at Replika Press Pvt. Ltd, India

This book is sold subject to the condition that it shall not, by way of trade
or otherwise, be lent, resold, hired out, or otherwise circulated without the
publisher's prior consent in any form of binding or cover other than that in
which it is published and without a similar condition including this condition
being imposed on the subsequent purchaser.

www.penguin.co.in

Disclaimer

The content of this book and the ideas expressed therein solely belong to the authors. The information provided should not be treated as recommendations for trading and investing in financial instruments. Some of the stocks mentioned may be held by the authors and/or their employers but are not recommendations for trading and investing. Readers should conduct thorough research before acting on any information presented as market data is subject to change and its accuracy cannot be guaranteed. This book is for informational purposes only and does not constitute a solicitation for financial transactions. Reproduction of confidential information is prohibited without the authors' consent. The opinions, figures and data included in the book are subject to change without notice. The authors make no warranties regarding the accuracy of the information presented, and readers are encouraged to verify facts independently. As past performance does not guarantee future results, the authors are not liable for losses resulting from investment and/or trading decisions made based on the book.

Contents

The more you dabble in the stock market, the luckier you will get. It is the only place where people think of changing their life without changing their actions.

—Pankaj Ladha

As you begin to read this book, just remember, if you think you can achieve it, you are right. On the other hand, if you think you can't, you are still right.

Your thoughts will define your actions, and your actions will define the result. So first focus on your thoughts, and things will start to fall in place.

—Anant Ladha

Part 1

An Overview of the Indian Stock Market

Chapter 1

Introduction to the Indian Stock Market

Friends, I have a story to tell you. A story which has been spun out of many dreams and has been written over decades. This is a story about the Indian economy and one of its strongest pillars, the capital markets. This is a journey that started decades ago and which, decades later, became a symbol of India's growth. Let us begin with it and understand how a trading activity taking place under a banyan tree became the seed of world financial system.

Overview of the Indian Economy and Its Relationship to the Stock Market

For a long period of time, stock markets in India have largely been an unfocused market for financial activities and were treated as a less important subject of finance. Traditional financing systems like banks in urban areas and moneylenders in rural areas had been controlling the Indian financial system. The opening up of the Indian economy and the emergence of the need for larger and improved capital-raising avenues brought the stock markets into the limelight. With time, the business started resizing itself and Indian markets saw the emergence of new-age enterprises like Reliance, L&T, HDFC and many more. These were the business enterprises which were not built with the help of money loaned by the family but with structured finance raised from capital and debt markets. Gradually, other entrepreneurs were inspired and wanted to join the race for creating larger organizations.

India has always had abundant finance but only a few had access to it. This caused the new-age entrepreneurs to struggle for finance. Debt funding was available, but collateral was always a problem for new entrepreneurs. At this stage, Indians needed structured and regulated capital raising systems which could work at the speed of thought. These systems evolved into the current generation of stock markets where trades and transactions are happening at the speed of thought. Companies are raising lakhs of crores in a day and secondary markets are stronger than ever. As I write this book, the average daily turnover at NSE alone is more than Rs 50,000 crore. Beyond this, Indian stock markets roughly contribute Rs 20,000 crore of STT (Securities Transaction Tax) annually to the government's treasury.

On the other hand, for some years, the stock markets have also been infamous but overall, these have been a great place to raise capital for companies and generate returns for investors. In this chapter, we will understand the basics of the Indian stock markets and recognize how they are related to various aspects of the economy.

The history of Indian stock markets: The Indian stock market is one of the oldest stock markets in Asia, with the Bombay Stock Exchange (BSE) being established in 1875. More recently, the National Stock Exchange (NSE), established in 1992, is India's largest stock market in terms of trading volume. On the regulatory front, the Indian stock markets are regulated by the Securities and Exchange Board of India (SEBI). It is important to state here that the strengthening of SEBI was a consequence of the need to counter the incidence of various scams which had arisen due to the absence of regulations in the markets.

The size of the Indian economy and its place in the world: After approximately 150 years of colonization and many years of toil post-Independence, the Indian economy has finally arrived at its rightful place. If we consider recent data relating to the Indian economy in absolute terms of Gross Domestic Product (GDP) we rank fifth in the world with nearly $3.75 trillion of GDP. By certain assumptions, it will very soon overtake Germany and Japan to become the third largest economy of the world, trailing just behind the USA and China.

Getting away from the absolute GDP, there is another method by which we can assess it, the Purchasing Power Parity (Model). If we consider the size of the Indian economy by this method, we can proudly say that we are the third largest in the world. The following graphical representation will show you the composition of the sectoral GDP. Here, we can draw a comparison with the earlier composition of the Indian economy, where agriculture used to have the lion's share. Now we see that the service sector is taking the lead. This can be seen at the company level too. Reliance, the largest Indian enterprise which was formerly only an oil and chemical producing company and generated 70 per cent of its revenue from the O2C [Order to Cash] business, now generates around 55 per cent from O2C and 15 per cent from Jioplatforms, a service company.

The Structure: We keep hearing that India is a diverse country and that there are many countries within it. The culture, language and behaviour are so diverse that India is a world unto itself. The same is true of the Indian economy. We are a mixed type of economy which means that both the government and the common public can own and operate a business. On the one hand, you find SBI, BOB and PNB, and on the other hand, you find HDFC and ICICI ruling the Indian financial markets. The coexistence of the public and private sector in India is evident in almost every sector, and the private sector is growing. As I write this chapter, we come to the following conclusion on considering data from the top 100 listed companies:

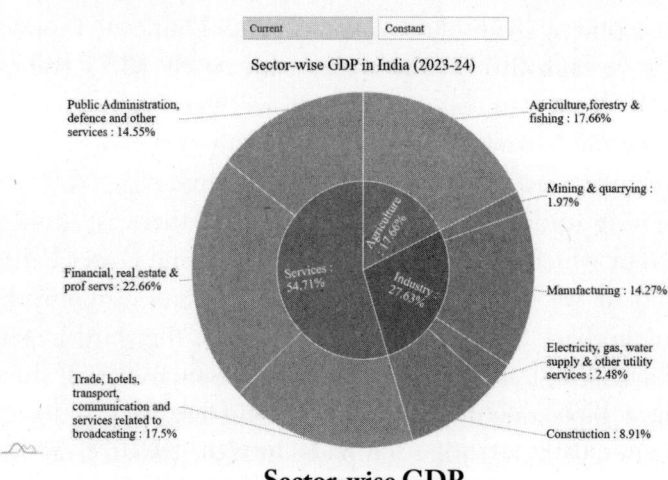

Sector-wise GDP

Source: statisticstimes.com

Type of company	Number	Sum of market capitalization as on 31 March 2023 (Rs in lakh)
Government	14	20,36,623
Private	86	1,55,88,365

It is clear that 88 per cent of the market capitalization of the top 100 listed companies are dominated by private players, while government-owned companies comprise only 12 per cent.

But things were different in the past. A study of the history of the post-Independence era shows that most resources and businesses were controlled by the government, and the production of most of the goods was licence-based. Around 1991, the government realized the importance of private participation in the growth of the country, and private companies were allowed to do business in areas such as banking, insurance, telecom, etc. That was the genesis of today's giants such as Bharti Airtel, Adani, HDFC Bank and others. Decades after we first embarked on liberalization, we can now see that growth where products and services are both easily available. The then prime minister and finance minister had realized then that to handle the current foreign currency crisis and to ensure the future global growth of the country, they would have to open up the economy and bring in greater capital flows.

In the early years, the Indian economy was largely based on an agrarian system. The volume of production was so low that customers had to wait at least four to five years to get delivery of a Bajaj scooter; an equally long wait was in store for those seeking a BSNL connection. Most industrial products were either unavailable or imported from foreign countries. Once the private sector was allowed to start businesses in various segments of the economy, the production of commodities like cement, steel, etc. began in India. Over the last twenty years, the pattern of the economy changed further and the bulk of it is now with the service sector.

We keep hearing about the growth rate of the GDP. In simple words, if, in a year, the economy produced goods worth Rs 100 and, in the following year, the total value of the goods produced is Rs 107, then the growth rate of the GDP is 7 per cent. If we talk about the current scenario in the world, then India is a high-growth market where the developed world is either facing degrowth or growing in the range of 2–3 per cent, Indian GPD is easily clocking a growth rate of 6–7 per cent per annum. The biggest reason behind such a growth rate is the demographic dividend that India enjoys.

A large part of the Indian population is under thirty-five years of age; this is driving consumption and spurring increased production.

The connection between the economy and markets: Technically speaking, stock markets are always a reflection of what is happening in the underlying economy. They are a reliable economic indicator, being the outcome of various tests borne by the national economy. For example, we can say that if the economy is suffering from higher inflation, then the stocks of banking companies will always tend to fall as there will be a fear that interest rates might be raised by the Reserve Bank of India (RBI). Due to higher inflation, RBI started raising rates from May 2022; the repo rate has now risen at the level of 6.5 per cent. Moreover, since the rate hikes started, stock markets are in range-bound trade.

The mathematics is simple. Since the stock market comprises the companies listed on it and because these business entities are working in the economy, any economic change will impact the financials of these companies and will finally be reflected in the stock prices. In any case, no company can be isolated from the economic performance of the nation. If the government raises the Goods and Services Tax (GST) rate on restaurants, it results in reduced consumption, which results in the fall of stocks like Burger King, Westlife, Devyani International and many more listed companies.

In other words, we can say that the stock markets are a kind of economic indicator, a well-performing stock market indicates that either the economy is doing well or that it is expected to do well in the upcoming days. For example, if FMCG stocks are performing well, it means that the consumption in the economy is good and that people are earning enough money to spend.

Recently ITC went beyond 400; this is a classic example of this scenario.

Another example is related to major economic events which leave an impact on stock markets. If we see the major global financial crisis of 2008, Indian stock markets lost almost 70 per cent of their value. A lot of stocks lost more than 90 per cent. The Sensex, which touched a high of 21,700, went up to 8800 during the crisis. Another major economic crisis of recent times was COVID-19 where the markets nosedived and lost almost half their value within a few days. Both these events reflected the strong connection between economic factors and stock markets.

Foreign investment and markets: Foreign investment plays a significant role in the Indian stock market. Foreign institutional investors (FIIs) are allowed to invest in the Indian stock market, subject to certain regulations. The better the volume and type of FII in markets like India, the higher the possibility of performance. For a number of years now, the Indian government has been working hard to bring in various policy changes to attract Foreign direct investment (FDI) and FII in Indian markets. It has opened various sectors from defence to retail for private and foreign investment. Here we need to understand that FDI creates a long-term positive impact on the market and FII buying shows an instant reaction in the prices of stocks. The following chart shows the quantum of FDI inflows in India. The trajectory is only upwards, clearly impacting the movement of the stock markets. We can see that the largest amount of FDI has come into information technology (IT). This created a huge business of small and mid-cap IT firms. The adjacent graph shows the NIFTY IT index. We can clearly see a correlation; the index has almost doubled since 2017.

(Updated up to September, 2024)

I.   CUMULATIVE FDI FLOWS INTO INDIA (2000-2024):

A.   TOTAL FDI INFLOW (from April, 2000 to September, 2024):

1	CUMULATIVE AMOUNT OF FDI INFLOW (Equity inflow +'Re-invested earnings' +'Other capital')		USD 1,033,400 Million
2	CUMULATIVE AMOUNT OF FDI EQUITY INFLOW (excluding, amount remitted through RBI's NRI Schemes)	INR 45,96,034 Crore	USD 708,654 Million

B.   FDI INFLOW DURING SECOND QUARTER OF FINANCIAL YEAR 2024-25 (JULY, 2024 TO SEPTEMBER, 2024):

1	TOTAL FDI INFLOW INTO INDIA (Equity inflow + 'Re-invested earnings' + 'Other capital') (as per RBI's Monthly bulletins)		USD 19,815 Million
2	FDI EQUITY INFLOW	INR 1,14,074 Crore	USD 13,813 Million

E.   SECTORS ATTRACTING HIGHEST FDI EQUITY INFLOW

Rank	Sector	Amt. in Rupees Crores/ Amt. in USD Million	2022-23 (April-March)	2023-24 (April-March)	2024-25 (April-Sept)	Cumulative Equity Inflow * (April, 2000-Sept, 2024)	%age out of total FDI Equity inflow (in terms of USD)
1	SERVICES SECTOR **	Rupees Crores	69,852	54,894	47,540	7,34,419	
		USD Million	8,707	6,640	5,692	115,188	16%
2	COMPUTER SOFTWARE & HARDWARE	Rupees Crores	74,718	66,090	35,025	7,53,894	
		USD Million	9,394	7,973	4,193	107,077	15%
3	TRADING	Rupees Crores	38,060	32,080	22,800	3,22,059	
		USD Million	4,792	3,865	2,722	46,118	7%
4	TELECOMMUNICATIONS	Rupees Crores	5,469	2,318	5,600	2,40,440	
		USD Million	713	282	670	39,996	6%
5	AUTOMOBILE INDUSTRY	Rupees Crores	15,184	12,622	7,889	2,43,176	
		USD Million	1,902	1,524	944	37,212	5%
6	CONSTRUCTION (INFRASTRUCTURE) ACTIVITIES	Rupees Crores	13,588	35,076	11,075	2,50,629	
		USD Million	1,703	4,232	1,324	35,242	5%
7	CONSTRUCTION DEVELOPMENT: Townships, housing, built-up infrastructure and construction-development projects	Rupees Crores	1,196	2,113	1,280	1,32,601	
		USD Million	147	255	153	26,764	4%
8	DRUGS & PHARMACEUTICALS	Rupees Crores	16,654	8,844	4,349	1,39,230	
		USD Million	2,058	1,064	520	23,048	3%
9	CHEMICALS (OTHER THAN FERTILIZERS)	Rupees Crores	14,662	6,985	6,070	1,39,774	
		USD Million	1,850	844	727	22,873	3%
10	NON-CONVENTIONAL ENERGY	Rupees Crores	19,977	31,188	17,531	1,43,692	
		USD Million	2,500	3,764	2,096	19,984	3%

Foreign Investments

Source: www.india-briefing.com

The power of retail investors: For a number of years, retail investors have been mere spectators in the stock markets. But now, their size and muscle power are growing day by day. The participation of retail investors in the Indian stock market has been increasing in recent years through direct equity investment or via pool investment tools like mutual funds. On a good note, the government has always been supportive by providing tax deductions for tools like Equity Linked Savings Schemes (ELSS) and Unit Linked Insurance Plan (ULIP). You will be amazed to know that India holds around twelve crore demat accounts now; the growth of demat holders is more than 30 per cent Year-over-Year.

Finally, we can say that stock markets in India are an important pillar of the economy and that the economy's performance impacts market valuations. Both are so interlinked that it is important for every investor to understand the functioning and the interlinking.

Historical Evolution of the Indian Stock Market

The history of Indian stock markets dates back to 1875, when the Bombay Stock Exchange, the oldest stock exchange in Asia, was established. Since then, Indian markets have gone through many changes and many events, both good and bad. In the upcoming pages, let us have a look back on the history of stock markets in India.

The early years: The Indian stock market can trace its roots back to the 1830s, when trading in shares of the East India Company began. The first formal stock exchange in India, BSE, was established in 1875. The BSE was primarily established to serve the interests of European merchants who were active in India at the time. We can say that the markets were not meant for the general public but were meant to serve only a few organizations and influential people.

Time would bring about changes in the market structure. The early years of the BSE were marked by limited activity and low trading volumes. The exchange grew in prominence in the early twentieth century, with the number of listed companies increasing steadily. The reason was the growth of the Indian economy and the need for finance to fuel this growth. The best place to raise long-term funding was the stock markets. Here is some of the data on Indian stock markets, which will tell you how it has been growing over the years. The need for finance led to the growth of stock markets in India and the rest is history. We can clearly see from the graphs how

Indian stock markets, in terms of both investors and investees, have thrived.

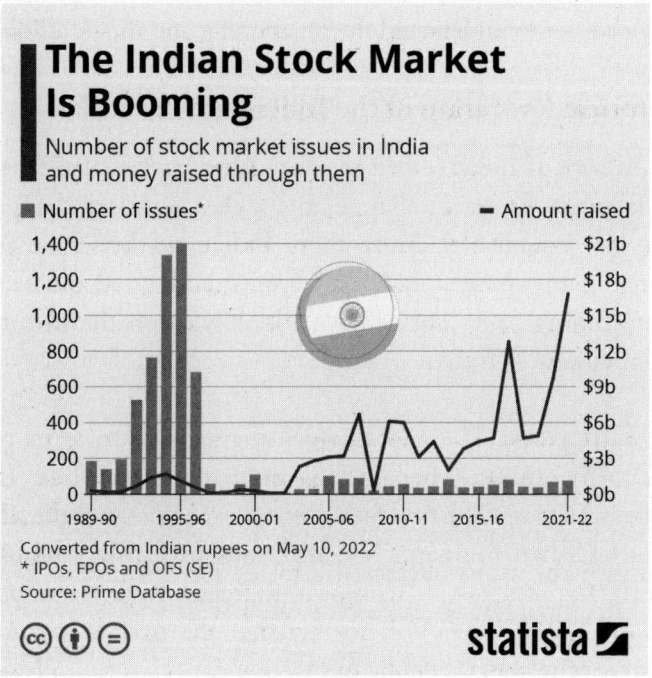

The Early Years

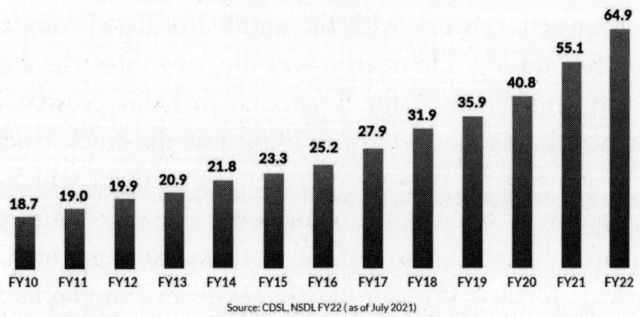

Depository Growth

Post-Independence era: The early years of the Indian stock markets were not exciting as the entire economy was struggling on account of resource and production scarcity. Most of the large industries were operated by the government and the growth in the industries was limited as the demand in the markets was also limited. But in the 1960s and 1970s, the Indian stock market witnessed significant growth, with the number of listed companies increasing rapidly. In 1964, the Delhi Stock Exchange was established, followed by the Calcutta Stock Exchange in 1978. This was a good move but since all these stock exchanges were regional, the market could not be developed well.

Liberalization and reforms: The year 1991 was a landmark in the history of the Indian economy. The government came up with the policy of LPG i.e., Liberalization, Privatization and Globalization. The government started opening the economy to private and global players. This not only fuelled local growth, it also attracted a lot of foreign investments in Indian companies. A spree of FDI, FII and local investment served as the genesis of the large organizations of today. There was an increase in the manufacturing/production of goods and the availability of services in the market. This in turn enhanced consumption and ushered in a cycle of economic growth and prosperity. The establishment of factories and facilities called for more investment and stock markets became the best place to raise capital. As a result, in the late 1990s and early 2000s, the Indian stock market witnessed significant growth, with the market capitalization of listed companies increasing rapidly. In 2000, the BSE Sensex, an index tracking the performance of the top 30 companies listed on the BSE, crossed the 5000 mark for the first time.

Global financial crisis: In recent times, this was one of the most impactful economic events. The global meltdown started with the sub-prime crisis in the USA which ultimately affected almost the entire world. The global financial crisis of 2008 had a significant impact on the Indian stock market. The market witnessed a sharp decline in 2008, with the BSE Sensex falling by around 50 per cent. The following graph shows that in the US alone, around 500 companies went bankrupt in 2008 and 2009. The crisis was so deep that it has even been compared to the Great Depression of 1929.

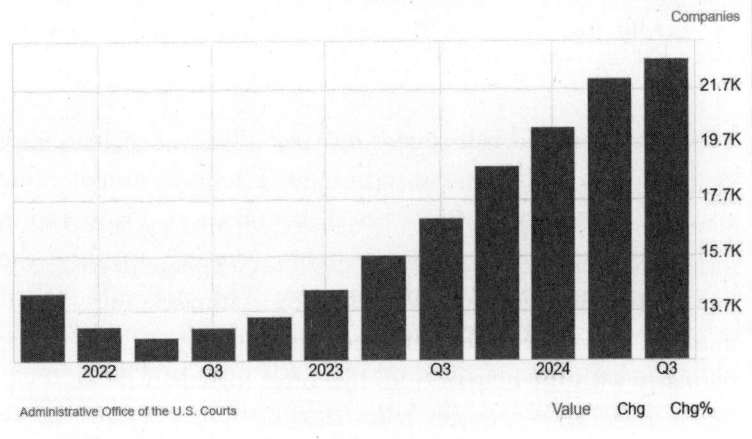

Global Financial Crisis

Source: tradingeconomics.com

However, the Indian stock market recovered quickly, with the Sensex crossing the 20,000 mark in 2010. One good thing about this global shock is that the world economies learnt how to control the overall financial system. Central banks around the globe became more vigilant about the financial system and lending practices around the world improved.

Recent developments: We can firmly say that the current period is one of the best for Indian stock markets. Stock trading and awareness about the markets are at an all-time high. Participation from retail is at its best, with the market capitalization of listed companies reaching new highs. As of now, there are more than 2000 companies listed on the Indian stock markets with a total market cap of over $5 trillion. Indian markets are now truly global in terms of technology platforms with both large stock markets, namely, NSE and BSE, leveraging improved technology day by day.

It is quite evident that the Indian stock market has come a long way since its early days in the nineteenth century. The market has witnessed significant growth and has played a key role in the growth of the Indian economy. The best part about today's markets is the growing participation from retail, an industry which had been quiet for many years. The markets have become huge wealth creators. With the retail fraternity, another participant which has gained thanks to the market momentum is the government. Divestment plans for the last few years have been successful due to a fantastic rally in the markets. The government has been successful in raising money regularly with the help of tools like offer for sale (OFS).

Key Players in the Indian Stock Market, Including Exchanges, Brokers and Regulators

The stock markets are just like any other market where different participants play a variety of roles. Just like a normal market, where there are buyers, sellers, brokers, etc. performing their roles, stock markets too work under the same principles. Being a financial market, it works under a lot of regulations. In the upcoming pages, we will try to understand the type and role of different market participants in the stock markets.

Exchanges: The most important part of the Indian stock market is the market itself which, in technical language, is called the Exchanges. It is the place where buying and selling takes place. India has two major exchanges—BSE and NSE. Both have their headquarters in Mumbai besides offices in other parts of the country. Both exchanges offer a range of products, including equities, derivatives and commodities. If we see the exchanges in the current scenario, we can say that these are nothing but fintechs providing technology services to the market participants. Currently, India has seven recognized stock exchanges.

Brokers: Stock markets are highly regulated and need a particular structure for every trade to take place. Brokers play a crucial role in facilitating transactions in the Indian stock market. Brokers can be categorized into two types—full-service brokers and discount brokers. Full-service brokers offer a range of services, including research and advisory services, while discount brokers charge low brokerage fees but offer limited services. Nowadays, with the enhanced level of knowledge in the market, discount brokerage houses are trending as it is easy to open and operate one's trading account with them. A few examples of this service are Zerodha and Upstox. As of now, there are more than 4000 registered brokers in India.

Regulators: Undisputedly, the most important part of the markets is the regulator. It decides everything about the markets, from raising money to trading. The regulator decides the rules and regulations of the markets. SEBI is the primary regulator of the Indian stock market. Established in 1988, SEBI is responsible for regulating the securities market in India. It is to be noted that initially, SEBI did not have much power. In 1992, when the biggest scam of the stock markets struck the economy, SEBI was given the status of sole and strongest regulator for the stock markets. SEBI's primary functions include regulating the stock exchanges, protecting investors and enforcing regulations to ensure fair and transparent trading practices.

Beyond SEBI, RBI also plays an important part in regulating stock markets indirectly as foreign funds are involved. FDI and Foreign Portfolio Investment (FPI) must take RBI approval before getting registered as stock market investors. Sometimes, there are regulatory conflicts; in such cases, the ministry has to get involved. One such conflict happened between SEBI and the Insurance Regulatory and Development Authority (IRDA) in 2010 when SEBI sent a show-cause notice to all life insurance companies, including the biggest player, Life Insurance Corporation (LIC), that sell this product. The insurers were asked to explain why they had not taken its approval before selling ULIPs. Finally, after the intervention of the government, it was announced that companies need IRDA approval only.

Investors/Traders: Investors and traders are the key players in the Indian stock market. These are the people who are the raison d'être of the markets. They buy and sell the instruments listed in the markets. They can be categorized into two types—institutional and retail investors, and traders. Institutional ones, such as mutual funds and insurance companies, account for a significant proportion of trading activity in the Indian stock market. Retail, on the other hand, includes individual investors who trade in the stock market through brokers. Here, we must understand that the institutional participants are the ones who dominate the markets in terms of volume and ownership. Their influence over the markets, in terms of pricing, is always the highest.

Market intermediaries: Market intermediaries play a crucial role in the Indian stock market by facilitating transactions between buyers and sellers. Market intermediaries include depository participants, clearing corporations and custodians. They are basically the back-end service providers to the buyer and seller. Depository participants are responsible for holding and maintaining securities in electronic form, while clearing corporations settle trades and ensure the timely delivery of securities. Though these are the back-end service providers to the market, it does not dilute the importance of market intermediaries. The quantum of innovation these companies have done in terms of technology and service speed is quite notable and now when we have moved from T+2 to T+1 settlement, and now even T+0, we can't negate the importance of intermediaries.

The Indian stock market is a complex ecosystem from the inside but provides a seamless experience to the user. This is largely possible due to the continuous innovation in terms of technology and processes. We need to understand that the importance of every market participant is as significant as the buyer and the seller in the market.

The charges that apply to you when you buy any stock in India:

1. **Brokerage fee:** This is the charge levied by the stock broker for transactions carried out by the investor based on the value of the contract or at a flat rate as agreed between the parties.

2. **STT:** This is a mandatory charge levied as a percentage. The STT rate is 0.1 per cent of the transaction value for delivery-based equity share trades.

3. **Stamp Duty and GST:** Stamp duty is charged by the state government as the transaction involves the transfer of security from one party to another. GST (Central and state GST) is levied as a percentage of the brokerage charged for the transaction. Currently, the rate is 9 per cent CGST and 9 per cent SGST.

4. **Transaction charge:** The stock exchange levies transaction charges on the buying and selling of shares at the rate decided by the respective stock exchange. SEBI charges a turnover fee of 0.0002 per cent of the transaction amount.

5. **Depository charge:** These charges are levied by the depository participant National Securities Depository

Ltd (NSDL) or Central Depository Services Ltd (CDSL) for safe-keeping of the securities of the investor.

6. **Capital gains tax:** Depending upon the holding period, tax is applicable on the profit earned from the sale of shares. The profit on the sale of shares held for less than one year is subject to short-term capital gains (STCG) and for one year or more is subject to long-term capital gains (LTCG) tax.

How do you place an order with your broker? Let's clarify the basics:

What Are Limit and Market Orders?

Limit orders are used to buy or sell an instrument at a specific price.
   Example scenario:

Buy limit order

Assume that the Current Market Price (CMP) of a share is Rs 95. The client wishes to buy when the price drops to Rs 90.

A buy limit order can be placed at Rs 90 and the stock will be bought at Rs 90 or lower.

Sell limit order

Assume that the CMP of a share is Rs 95. A client wishes to sell the share when the price is Rs 100.

A sell limit order can be placed at Rs 100 and the stock will be sold at Rs 100 or higher.

The advantage of a limit order is that the share is bought at the desired price. However, unless a counter order for the specified quantity or price is available, the order may not be completely fulfilled, resulting in partial execution.

Limit orders are valid only for one day. To place long-standing orders with a one-year validity, use Good Till Triggered (GTT) orders. The GTT feature is an order that

stays active until the trigger condition is met. The validity of the trigger is one year.

Market Orders

Market orders are used to buy or sell an instrument at the best available price. A buy market order purchases the share at any price available. Similarly, a sell market order sells the share at any price available. If there are counterparties, market orders can be executed immediately when they reach the exchange. However, because the order is executed instantly, the share may be purchased at a higher price or sold at a lower price.

As a retail investor, it is always preferable to use the limit order, rather than the market order, especially in the case of small caps to ensure a lower impact cost.

Market Structure and Participants

A family is made up of various members. In the same way, stock markets are also made up of members. In general, when we see the stock markets from an outside perspective, we see only buyers and sellers. But to understand the basics of the stock markets, we need to understand that there are many other activities which are done behind the scenes. It is like seeing the actors on the screen but we must remember that there are so many people behind the scenes. The dialogue at which you cheer is written by others. In the same way, there are many people and organizations working behind the scenes in the stock markets.

Structure of the Indian Stock Market, Including the Primary and Secondary Markets

Introduction: Many years ago, when I started trading, I used to think that it was easy to execute a trade. Just call the broker and buy or sell shares. But that's not all there is to it. Stock markets all around the world consist of a complex financial system. Since it involves the raising and trading of billions of dollars, it requires multiple layers of operations and regulations. The Indian stock market is no different. It comprises the primary market and the secondary market about which we will learn in the upcoming pages. We will also discuss the structure of the Indian stock market and the role of primary and secondary markets.

Primary market: The primary market is also known as the new issue market. Any company which wants to issue fresh capital can issue it through the primary market only. In the primary market, companies can issue instruments like equity shares, preference shares, debentures and bonds. In simple language, issuance is nothing but calling for investment from investors like retail and institutional investors. The companies can, under a fixed process, raise the amount from different types of investors. These investors are also of various categories like individual retail, individual HNI and institutional. To simplify the primary market in case of equity shares, we can term it IPO markets. When any company wants to issue shares to the general public or institutions, it must tap the primary markets.

Initial Public Offering (IPO) is the most common method used by companies to raise capital in the primary market. In an IPO, a company offers its shares to the public for the first time. The first process to begin for an IPO is to file a DRHP (Draft Red Herring Prospectus) with the market regulator, SEBI. In other words, DRHP is an application which contains all the information about the company's financial and non-financial activities. The purpose behind this document is that the investors must learn about various aspects of the company. Once SEBI approves of the DRHP, the company can go to market and raise money using due procedure. It is to be noted that the entire process of fundraising via IPO is completely governed by SEBI. The company cannot afford any deviation from it. Most of you would have invested in IPOs via your broker and must be aware about the process too.

Secondary Market: Once the securities are issued to investors, they would either like to sell or buy more of the same type. To do this, trading must take place and trading can be done in some market only. To fulfil this objective, secondary markets exist. They are usually called the stock exchange or the stock market. This is where securities are traded among investors. The secondary market provides a platform for investors to buy and sell securities previously issued in the primary market. The secondary market comprises two major exchanges—BSE and NSE. For example, we can say that the primary market is the farm where grain is produced and the secondary market is the grain market where various buyers and sellers come together to trade.

This is a platform where buyers and sellers interact and fulfil each other's requirements. Another important point to understand is why people buy or sell. Simply put, if you believe that a company will perform better in terms of financials and will be able to distribute better profits, you would want to own more of it. To buy more of it, you will have to go to the markets which are nothing but stock exchanges. On the other hand, if you believe that the company will not perform well, then you would want to get rid of the stock. To sell too, you need to go to the stock exchange.

For example, if I feel that going forward, the market is going to see a greater demand for speciality chemicals, then the inference is that companies like Vinati Organics and Tata Chemicals will benefit, and so I will want to buy more shares of these companies. At the same time, if I feel that the interest rates are going to be raised by RBI, then companies like DLF and Oberoi Realty will stand to lose. In that case, I would like to sell those shares. In both scenarios, I will need a market called the stock markets.

Another important point is that the secondary market offers liquidity to investors, allowing them to buy and sell securities at market-determined prices. The prices are simply an action of the demand and supply of the stock in the markets. The reason for the demand and supply has already been discussed in the earlier paragraph.

The entire secondary market is also regulated by SEBI. SEBI ensures that the market operates in a transparent and fair manner and takes measures to protect the interests of investors. The regulator must take care of the interests of all parties while regulating the stock markets. As we have seen in the early years of stock markets, the absence of regulation has done a lot of damage to the investor community. Since 1992 however, the stock markets in India have not seen any major irregularity in trading activities. Rather, SEBI has been quite prompt in punishing wrongdoers.

Primary and secondary markets are the basic building blocks of the market. The yearly issuance of securities and the daily trading volume of the markets depend on current market conditions. In recent times, we have seen that post-COVID-19, the stock market boom has created a flurry of IPOs in the market and the daily trading volume has jumped by a huge percentage.

Types of Participants, Including Retail Investors, Institutional Investors and Foreign Investors

Any market is incomplete without the participants in it. The same is the case with stock markets. These participants are the market makers; the market exists because of them alone. The Indian stock market has a wide range of participants, including retail investors, institutional investors and foreign investors. In this section, we will discuss the types of participants in the Indian stock market.

Retail investors: Retail investors are individual investors who invest in the stock market through brokers. They are basically small investors who get into the markets to invest their routine savings and see some long-term appreciation. In general, retail investors do not have sufficient knowledge and time to track the market. That is why they either invest in markets via tools like mutual funds or consult their broker before investing in stocks. The risk appetite of retail investors is always lower as they enter the market with their savings.

Retail investors can participate in the Indian stock market by opening a demat account with a broker. This is an electronic account that holds securities in digital form. Investors can buy and sell securities in the secondary market through their demat accounts. In recent times, the amount of trading and investing done by retail investors has gone up sharply. The number of demat accounts held by retail investors is at an all-time high of close to 13 crore.

Institutional investors: Institutional investors are large investors who invest in the stock market on behalf of their clients. They include mutual funds, insurance companies, pension funds and hedge funds. Institutional investors account for a significant proportion of trading activity in the Indian stock market. They are basically the market makers and invest in stocks in bulk. On the other side, they also sell in bulk. The activity of institutional investors largely decides the way the market moves. The biggest institutional investor in India is LIC, which holds shares worth Rs 10 lakh crore on behalf of its policyholders.

The risk appetite of institutional investors is comparatively higher as a particular stock in their overall portfolio does not account for a big part of the whole. Due to this, they can invest aggressively in volatile and risky stocks too. It is notable that the great price appreciation on stocks since the 2005 rally in the market is largely due to higher institutional activities.

Foreign investors: Foreign investors are non-resident investors who invest in the Indian stock market. Foreign investors can invest in the Indian stock market through the FPI route. FPIs are typically institutional investors who invest in the Indian stock market on behalf of their clients. These are large funds with a huge amount of investible money. The basic reason why foreign funds will invest in any market is the falling rate of interest or less attractive domestic markets. As we have seen, till mid-2022, the rate of interest in major markets like the USA, Japan and European countries has been continuously falling. As a result, Indian markets have seen a huge influx of money invested by FIIs. As India is still an emerging market, it is expected to attract a larger amount of money from FIIs in the coming years. If we take the reverse case of higher interest rates, then the money will flow out of the equity markets and will be parked in instruments like fixed deposits.

The Indian stock market has a wide range of participants, including retail investors, institutional investors and foreign investors. Each participant plays a crucial role in ensuring the smooth functioning of the market. The participation of institutional and foreign investors has increased significantly in recent years, and the Indian stock market has witnessed significant growth as a result. The best thing about the increased participation of institutional investors is that Indian markets have gained amazingly and the retail investor has been able to make a lot of money. The Sensex, which was barely at 9000 in 2005, is now over 80,000, which is a great 11 per cent CAGR [compounded annual growth rate]. This was largely possible due to increased institutional interest in the Indian markets.

Role of Market Makers, Market Regulators and Other Intermediaries

The Indian stock market comprises various intermediaries who facilitate trading and ensure the smooth functioning of the market. In this section, we will discuss the role of market makers, market regulators and other intermediaries in the markets. It is quite notable that in the past few years, due to the enhanced participation of retail and institutional investors, the role of the participants, especially that of the regulators, has become very important.

Market makers: Market makers are intermediaries who provide liquidity to the market by buying and selling securities. Market makers ensure that there is a continuous flow of orders in the market, thereby providing liquidity to investors. In the Indian stock market, market makers are typically brokerage firms or investment banks. These brokerage firms play a crucial role in educating their clients about the markets. This in turn translates into the trading volume. The retail investor is largely dependent on the advisory supplied by these market makers. They need to be quite vigilant about the activities of the markets and ensure that the clients get the best of services and information on time.

In recent times, we have seen that brokerage firms not only provide brokerage services but do a lot of market research too. Top brokerage firms like Zerodha, Upstox, Angel, etc., keep generating daily reports which provide traders a base for trading. Based on these reports, traders either buy or sell the stock.

Market regulators: Market regulators are intermediaries who regulate the stock market to ensure that it operates in a transparent and fair manner. SEBI regulates the primary and secondary markets and ensures that companies and market participants follow the necessary disclosure norms and adhere to the regulatory framework. To ensure this, SEBI regularly comes up with various reporting formats and notifications. Beyond this, SEBI officials keep monitoring the trading practices undertaken by the market participants. In case anything beyond the law is found, the regulator can take necessary action.

SEBI also takes measures to protect the interests of investors and promotes the development of the Indian stock market. Other market regulators in India include RBI, which regulates banking and financial services, and the Ministry of Corporate Affairs (MCA), which regulates corporate affairs in India.

Beyond regulating the markets, SEBI is given the task of educating the nation about the securities markets. For this purpose, SEBI has established the National Institute of Securities Markets (NISM) which works in the field of financial education and certifications.

Other intermediaries: Other intermediaries in the Indian stock market include brokers, depository participants (DPs) and custodians. Brokers are intermediaries who facilitate trading in the stock market by executing buy and sell orders on behalf of clients. DPs hold securities in electronic form in demat accounts, while custodians hold securities on behalf of institutional investors. Of these, DPs and custodians are like back-end service providers to ensure that post-trade activities are conducted smoothly.

Every entity whose role has been discussed above has its own importance in the stock market. The absence of even one of these will break the chain of transparency, regulation and convenience. Regulators, brokers and traders are the face of the stock markets and DPs, the clearing agency and custodians are the back-end service providers. The best part about the overall structure is that there is no overlapping of any role; every participant works well in their own area.

Market Instruments

If we have markets, we also need goods to trade in it. As we know, the stock market is a place where securities can be traded. Earlier these securities were traded in physical paper mode. Thanks to the evolution of technology, software has taken place of open outcry. Computers have taken the place of physical markets. The stock exchanges are now financial technology companies rather than markets, as understood traditionally. Let us now understand the various types of market instruments used in the stock markets.

Types of Securities Traded on the Indian Stock Market, Including Stocks, Bonds and Derivatives

Stocks: Stocks, also known as equities, represent ownership in a company. When an investor buys a stock, he becomes a shareholder in the company and has a claim on the company's assets and earnings. This claim is notional and not at wish. For example, if you hold 1 per cent in Tata Motors, you cannot wake up on a good day and tell the company that they should give you money or any other asset equal to 1 per cent shareholding. You will be given the share in the company's profit as dividend only. In the Indian stock market, stocks are traded on NSE and BSE. Beyond these, India has certain regional stock exchanges also but as per the trading perspective, these markets are not very relevant.

The Indian stock market has a wide range of stocks available for trading, including large-cap, mid-cap, and small-cap stocks. Large-cap stocks are stocks of large, established companies, while mid-cap and small-cap stocks are stocks of smaller companies with higher growth potential. Largely, while discussing the category of the stocks, we categorize these as per their market cap, which means total market value. To arrive at the market value, we use the formula, total stocks outstanding*price per share. It is to be noted that the market cap keeps fluctuating with changes in the price per share. Today's small cap can be tomorrow's large cap or vice versa.

SEBI defines large-cap companies as those listed companies which are ranked from 1st to 100th on the Indian stock exchange in terms of market capitalization. Mid-cap companies are ranked from 101 to 250 in terms of market capitalization and small-cap companies start from the 251st rank. The following are some of the examples of stocks under various categories.

Symbol	Company Name	Market capitalization as on 31 March 2023 (Rs in Lakh)	Category
RELIANCE	Reliance Industries Limited	15,77,069	Large Cap
INFY	Infosys Limited	5,92,394	Large Cap
HDFC	Housing Development Finance Corporation Limited	4,80,483	Large Cap
LICI	Life Insurance Corporation of India	3,37,976	Large Cap
AXISBANK	Axis Bank Limited	2,64,121	Large Cap

MOTHERSON	Samvardhana Motherson International Limited	45,470	Mid Cap
PAGEIND	Page Industries Limited	42,277	Mid Cap
ABCAPITAL	Aditya Birla Capital Limited	37,128	Mid Cap
LTTS	L&T Technology Services Limited	35,678	Mid Cap
LINDEINDIA	Linde India Limited	34,368	Mid Cap
KEC	KEC International Limited	11,732	Small Cap
GALAXYSURF	Galaxy Surfactants Limited	8259	Small Cap
KNRCON	KNR Constructions Limited	7135	Small Cap
GALLANTT	Gallantt Ispat Limited	1343	Small Cap
HERITGFOOD	Heritage Foods Limited	1338	Small Cap

The above classification is based on current data. The actual status will keep changing as per the market performance of stocks.

Bonds: Bonds are debt securities that represent a loan to the issuer of the bond. When investors buy a bond, they are basically lending money to the issuer of the bond and receiving interest payments in return. These are fixed return instruments and less risky compared to equity. As the returns are fixed, these instruments suit those investors who want lower risk and moderate returns from their investments. Typically, bonds are quite similar to the fixed deposits of banks where the investor gets fixed returns and the investments are protected by guarantee. Here I would like to bust a myth that bonds are not risky. We can say that there is lower risk compared to equity, but the risk of default is already there in bonds issued by private parties. The following is a chart depicting the size of the Indian bond market.

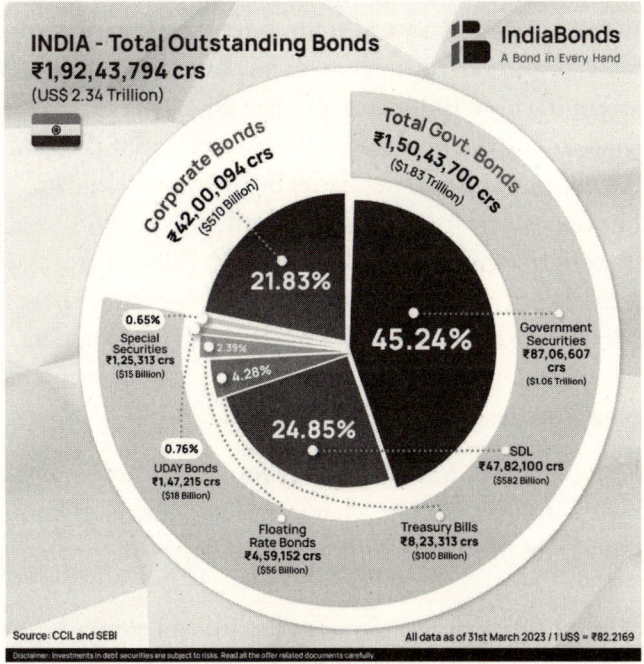

Bonds

The Indian bond market has a wide range of bonds available for trading, including government bonds, corporate bonds and municipal bonds. Government bonds are issued by the Central or state governments, while corporate bonds are issued by companies to raise capital. Municipal bonds are issued by local governments to finance infrastructure projects. The most famous type of traded bonds are government bonds and corporate bonds.

Derivatives: Derivatives are financial instruments that derive their value from an underlying asset. There are two types of derivatives traded in the Indian stock market: **futures and options**.

Futures: A futures contract is a legally binding agreement between two parties to buy or sell an asset at a predetermined price on a specific future date. The asset can be a commodity, such as oil or gold, or a financial instrument, such as a stock index or currency pair. When you buy a futures contract, you are agreeing to buy the asset at the agreed-upon price on the expiration date, regardless of the current market price. For example, if you buy a futures contract for 100 barrels of oil at Rs 50 per barrel, you are obligated to buy the oil for Rs 50 per barrel, even if the market price of oil rises to Rs 60 per barrel by the expiration date.

The opposite is true if you sell a futures contract. If you sell a futures contract for 100 barrels of oil at Rs 50 per barrel, you are obligated to sell the oil for Rs 50 per barrel even if the market price of oil falls to Rs 40 per barrel by the expiration date.

Types of Futures Contracts

There are many different types of futures contracts available, each with its own unique characteristics. Some of the most common types of futures contracts include:

Commodity futures: Commodity futures contracts involve the trading of physical commodities, such as oil, gold and corn.

Financial futures: Financial futures contracts involve the trading of financial instruments, such as stock indexes, currencies and interest rates.

Index futures: Index futures contracts track the performance of a specific market index, such as the Nifty or Bank Nifty.

Role of Margin and Leverage

Futures trading is a leveraged market, which means that you can control a large amount of an asset with a relatively small amount of capital. This is because futures contracts are settled in cash, not using physical assets.

Options: Options contracts are powerful financial tools that give you the option (but not the obligation) to buy or sell an asset at a specific price within a set time frame. They let you participate in the price movements of an underlying asset without actually owning it.

Example: Suppose you purchase a call option for the shares of Company XYZ at a strike price of Rs 1000 and an expiration date of three months. If the stock price rises above Rs 1000 within that time, you can exercise the option and buy the shares at the agreed-upon price, potentially making a profit. However, if the stock price remains below Rs 1000 or goes down, you have the choice not to exercise the option, limiting your loss to the premium you paid for the option.

Types

Call options: Think of call options as a ticket to buy something. When you buy a call option, you are acquiring the right to purchase the asset at a predetermined price before the expiration date. It's like having the option to buy a smartphone at a fixed price, even if its market value goes up.

Put options: On the other hand, put options give you the right to sell an asset at a predetermined price before the expiration date. It's like having the option to sell your old smartphone at a guaranteed price, even if its market value drops.

Basic Terms

Underlying security: Central to Futures and Options (F&O) trading, the value of derivatives hinges on the underlying security. This can encompass stocks, bonds, commodities, interest rates, indices or currencies.

Strike price: The agreed-upon price at which the contract owner or derivatives trader commits to buying or selling the derivative on a predetermined date.

Premium: The current option price paid by the buyer to the seller. Premiums rise with increased volatility in the underlying assets.

Expiry date: The specified date set by contract owners, signalling when traders must exercise their rights or obligations.

The growth of trading volumes in India's capital markets has been fantastic over the years. The growth can be seen in the following graph:

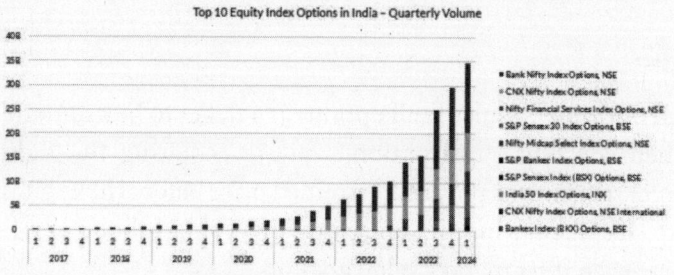

What Is Driving the Growth in Trading Volume?

In the first quarter of 2024, more than 34.8 equity index options traded on India's NSE and BSE. That was more than twice the total traded in Q1 2023, and more than 73% of all futures and options traded on all exchanges worldwide.

Growth in Trading Volume

Source: www.ndtvprofit.com

Whereas the growth in the cash and futures volumes has not been super exciting, NSE's options turnover has increased 50x from the 2015–22 period. Options turnover, which was 3x that of the combined Cash and Futures volumes in 2015, has increased to 70x in 2022.

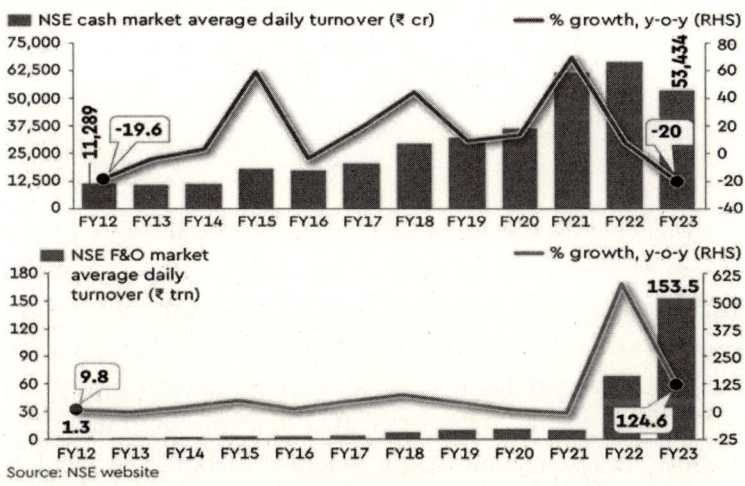

Turnover

Source: www.india-briefing.com

Chapter 2

Corporate Governance and Disclosure Practices

Transparency is key to success in any financial and business system. In the past, the world has seen so many financial scams just because of the lack of transparency. The most notorious scam around the world was Enron; in India, we have Satyam as an example. Transparency is a crucial element of a robust corporate governance system. It ensures that relevant information is disclosed in a timely and accurate manner, enabling stakeholders to make informed decisions. This transparency in simple working practices is called Corporate Governance. We can say that corporate governance is nothing but taking care of every part attached to the corporate. Corporate governance in India has undergone a significant overhaul since the late 1990s. In 2000, SEBI introduced the first set of comprehensive corporate governance reforms via Clause 49 of the listing agreement of stock exchanges. Over the period, the Companies Act, 2013 was enacted and a new set of corporate governance rules came into existence. In the image below, we can see how corporate governance has evolved in India.

CORPORATE GOVERNANCE IN INDIA
TIMELINE
civilspedia.com

1988	1992	1997	2006	2013	2017
SEBI was formed to regulate Security Markets	SEBI was given the Statutory status after Harshad Mehta Scam.	CII accepted there is need to strengthen Corporate Governance in India	Narayan Murthy Committee recommended strengthening Corporate Governance	Companies Act was amended to strengten Corporate Governance	Kotak Mahindra Committee recommended how to strengthen Corporate Governance

Corporate Governance

To understand corporate governance, we need to understand each of its elements better. We need to understand what is required at which level and how the overall picture of corporate governance is framed. At various points, the requirements of disclosure and regulations have changed. The elements of corporate governance include:

Board of Directors: This is where it starts. The top of the pyramid must be in full control of corporate governance. As we have seen in the case of some of the biggest corporate failures around the world like Enron, Satyam, etc., it all started from the top. First the top leadership went rogue, then the financial and other irregularities started. The Board of Directors is responsible for the overall governance and strategic direction of the company. It is composed of individuals with diverse backgrounds and expertise who oversee management, set policies and make important decisions. If the Board of Directors are not serious about the annual compliance of the company, then the compliance department will be helpless. One recent example is Byju's, which did not announce its profit and loss for around eighteen months. It did make an announcement later on but only when SEBI intervened. On the other hand, almost all the top league companies in India are quite serious about it and we can see that the annual financial statements are always declared on time.

Shareholder rights: Corporate governance and shareholder rights are quite interlinked. Both are essential in ensuring the smooth functioning of a company. Good corporate governance standards set the rules and regulations which give shareholders the right to participate in important business decisions. Though shareholders cannot directly participate in decisions as the company is operated by the top management, they can do so by voting for important decisions in the annual meet. Some of the important decisions are the appointment of board members, a review of the financials of the company and anything else which is considered important. Any shareholder can, at any time, raise objections to the available decision point or data. Good corporate governance and strong shareholder rights can help prevent mismanagement, fraud and other forms of unethical behaviour, and can enhance the reputation and stability of a company. Transparency in front of the shareholders ensures that their rights are protected.

Transparency and disclosure: Transparency and disclosure are two other important pillars of the corporate governance structure. Corporations must be transparent about their conduct and that transparency can only be brought about via various disclosure practices. Some of the disclosures are mandatory due to legal requirements offset in the Companies Act, etc. On the other hand, some of the disclosures are voluntary. For example, a listed company has to mandatorily disclose the following information on its website:

- Details of its business
- Terms and conditions of the appointment of independent directors
- Composition of various committees of the Board of Directors
- Code of Conduct of the Board of Directors and senior management personnel

- Details of the establishment of vigil mechanism/ whistle-blower policy
- Criteria for making payments to non-executive directors, if the same has not been disclosed in the annual report
- Policy on dealing with related party transactions
- Policy for determining 'material' subsidiaries

Any deviation from any legal disclosures shall lead to penalties or any other type of action. That is why companies should provide transparent and timely information to shareholders, investors and the public. This includes financial reporting, disclosure of material information and compliance with applicable laws and regulations. Annual or quarterly announcements of results is also a kind of disclosure from the corporate.

Beyond the regulatory disclosures, there are a lot of things which most companies disclose to the stakeholders on a voluntary basis. For example, Adani group companies have been reporting their Sustainability Report in BRSR (Business Responsibility and Sustainability Reporting) format even before it was made mandatory by SEBI. The overall purpose of the disclosure is to make the stakeholders more aware about the company they are connected to so that they can make an informed decision about every business activity with the entity.

Risk management: Corporate governance involves identifying and managing risks that may affect the company's performance, both in terms of financials and societal impact. Effective risk management systems are those which contain an internal control system to mitigate the overall business risk of the company. Within the corporate governance board structure, the role of overseeing risk management is usually that of the Audit Committee, and it may be shared by the Risk Committee, if the company has one. The Audit Committee keeps the system in place by keeping a check on the activities as decided in the planning documents. For instance, while investing in a business, the company must have overall financial control. In India, Kingfisher Airlines is one such example where the top management could not keep things under control. We all know what happened later. The management kept investing in the business, even when the losses went out of control.

Compliance and legal framework: Compliance is just abiding by the law and sharing the required information with the regulators and stakeholders. In India, compliance on the part of corporates is largely governed by the Companies Act, 2013, and in the case of listed entities, with the stock exchanges and SEBI playing an additional role. It is important that companies comply with the relevant laws, regulations and corporate governance guidelines. They should establish mechanisms to monitor and ensure compliance as well as manage legal and regulatory risks. Other than corporate level compliance, the business entity has to comply with statutory compliances like tax payments, labour laws, etc.

Compliance

Source: ikamate.com

Long-term sustainability: A corporate is a perpetual entity. The business and the company remain forever; the ownership might change. We have seen many examples in the global and Indian context where a single corporate entity has been under various owners over a period, but the business has sustained itself. Corporate governance focuses on the long-term sustainability and success of the company. It encourages a strategic approach that considers ESG factors, as well as the company's impact on society and the environment. These aspects of corporate governance lead the company on a sustainable journey.

Disclosure Requirements for Listed Companies Which Might Be Useful for You as an Investor

Listed companies affect a lot of stakeholders; the financial and non-financial activities of the listed companies have a large impact on various parts of the financial and social structure. This is why listed companies are required to disclose various financial and non-financial activities and decisions. The basic requirements around disclosure are that the information should reach the markets, and on that basis, the investor community will take a call on the investment and the regulators and other parties will make sure that things are going well within the companies. The reason why disclosure is required is because less information is always risky. There have been cases like Enron and Satyam Computers where limited information and poor disclosure practices destroyed investors' wealth and societal confidence due to less information and bad disclosure practices.

Financial reporting: The most important part of the disclosure for listed entities is the financial aspect. Listed companies are generally required to disclose their financial statements, including income statements, balance sheets, cash flow statements and accompanying notes in required formats. As a trader or investor, you would have seen that every quarter, companies have to come up with their financial results which are to be submitted on stock exchanges where the company is listed.

Annual reports: Listed companies also prepare and publish annual reports, which provide a comprehensive overview of the company's performance, financial condition, business strategy and risks. These reports may include the financial statements, management's discussion and analysis (MD&A), and other relevant information. The annual report of a company is an important document as it contains information that is not related to finances. It talks about the management's perspective and any future growth vision of the company.

Material events: Listed companies are generally required to promptly disclose any material events or information that could potentially impact their stock price. Any decision or event which is important for the company's financial and non-financial performance is to be disclosed by the company. Material events may include significant acquisitions or divestitures, changes in executive leadership, major litigation or regulatory developments that could affect the company's operations or financial condition. For example, if Reliance Industries has entered into an agreement to acquire another company, it will have to disclose the same on stock exchanges as it is important for the company's financials. If any company's CFO, CEO or any other KMP resigns from the company, that information must also be disclosed as it is important non-financial information. The following is a screenshot of a company from the BSE website where the disclosures made by the company are listed.

Company : Bajaj Housing Finance Ltd			
544252 | Updation In Details Under Regulation 30(5) Of The SEBI (Listing Obligations And Disclosure Requirements) Regulations, 2015	Company Update	0.41 MB	XBRL
Updation in details under Regulation 30(5) of the SEBI (Listing Obligations and Disclosure Requirements) Regulations, 2015			
Exchange Received Time 13-12-2024 12:34:50 Exchange Disseminated Time 13-12-2024 12:34:51 Time Taken 00:00:01			
544252 | Announcement under Regulation 30 (LODR)-Newspaper Publication	Company Update	1.87 MB	XBRL
Intimation under Regulation 30 and 47 of the SEBI (Listing Obligations and Disclosure Requirements) Regulations, 2015 - Newspaper Advertisement			
Exchange Received Time 22-11-2024 15:23:01 Exchange Disseminated Time 22-11-2024 15:23:01 Time Taken 00:00:00			
544252 | Submission Of Half-Yearly Report For FY2024-25	Company Update	2.49 MB	XBRL
Submission of Half-Yearly Report for FY2024-25 containing the financial performance of the Company including update on key developments during the half year ended 30 September 2024.			
Exchange Received Time 30-10-2024 22:41:58 Exchange Disseminated Time 30-10-2024 22:41:58 Time Taken 00:00:00			
544252 | Announcement under Regulation 30 (LODR)-Earnings Call Transcript	Company Update	0.49 MB	XBRL
Transcript of conference call for the quarter and half-year ended 30 September 2024.			
Exchange Received Time 25-10-2024 22:36:10 Exchange Disseminated Time 25-10-2024 22:36:10 Time Taken 00:00:00			
544252 | Announcement under Regulation 30 (LODR)-Monitoring Agency Report	Company Update	0.45 MB	XBRL
Monitoring agency report for the quarter ended 30 September 2024, in relation to the Public Issue of the Company.			
Exchange Received Time 24-10-2024 17:27:36 Exchange Disseminated Time 24-10-2024 17:27:36 Time Taken 00:00:00			

Announcements

Insider trading and shareholder disclosures: This is one of the most important aspects of the disclosures to be made by Indian listed companies. Listed companies often have obligations related to insider trading, which typically require insiders (such as directors, officers and significant shareholders) to disclose their trades in the company's securities. Those shareholders who have important positions and hold material shareholding in the company are generally termed insiders. In other words, the employees or other reported parties which have access to important insider information about the company have to follow certain rules and regulations regarding trading in the stock. They cannot trade freely like other common shareholders and must disclose trading in the stock. In the following image, you can see the insider trading disclosures made by the shareholders of Reliance Industries. Transactions initiated by the relatives of designated insiders are also to be disclosed over stock exchanges. Insider trading regulation is necessary because insiders can take advantage of any price sensitive information before it is published in the public domain.

Name to Person	Category of Person *	Securities held pre Transaction	Securities Acquired / Disposed			Transaction Type	Securities held post Transaction	Period ##	Mode of Acquisition #	Trading in Derivatives			Reported to Exchange
			Type of Securities	Number	Value					Type of Contract	Buy Value (Units~)	Sale Value (Units~)	
SANJEEV SEKSARIA	Immediate Relative	0 (0.00)	Equity Shares	40000	8778000.00	Acquisition	40000 (0.00)	14/02/2022 14/02/2022	Gift	-	-	-	18/02/2022
SANJEEV SEKSARIA	Immediate Relative	0 (0.00)	Equity Shares	40000	9290000.00	Acquisition	40000 (0.00)	10/02/2022 10/02/2022	Gift	-	-	-	15/02/2022
LN BALAJI	Immediate Relative	121710 (0.00)	Equity Shares	21500	5048338.00	Disposal	100210 (0.00)	10/12/2021 10/12/2021	Market Sale	-	-	-	13/12/2021
JAYANT AWASTHI	Immediate Relative	150000 (0.00)	Equity Shares	5000	1144000.00	Pledge	150000 (0.00)	09/11/2021 09/11/2021	Creation Of Pledge	-	-	-	12/11/2021
S RANGRASS	Immediate Relative	0 (0.00)	Equity Shares	20000	4531000.00	Acquisition	20000 (0.00)	02/11/2021 02/11/2021	Off Market	-	-	-	09/11/2021
ASHESH AMBASTA	Employee	187330 (0.00)	Equity Shares	25000	5352621.00	Disposal	162330 (0.00)	09/08/2021 09/08/2021	Market Sale	-	-	-	12/08/2021
BAPPADITYA RAY CHAUDHURI	Employee	246604 (0.00)	Equity Shares	30000	6390000.00	Disposal	216604 (0.00)	10/08/2021 10/08/2021	Market Sale	-	-	-	12/08/2021
DEBOJIT GHOSH	Employee	136385 (0.00)	Equity Shares	15500	3253731.00	Disposal	120885 (0.00)	10/08/2021 10/08/2021	Market Sale	-	-	-	12/08/2021
RAJIV TANDON	Director	165750 (0.00)	Equity Shares	20000	4336000.00	Disposal	145750 (0.00)	09/08/2021 09/08/2021	Market Sale	-	-	-	12/08/2021
SANDEEP KAUL	Employee	55000 (0.00)	Equity Shares	30000	6300000.00	Pledge	55000 (0.00)	10/08/2021 10/08/2021	Creation Of Pledge	-	-	-	12/08/2021
SANDIP DATTA	Employee	58025 (0.00)	Equity Shares	5000	1080000.00	Disposal	53025 (0.00)	09/08/2021 09/08/2021	Market Sale	-	-	-	12/08/2021

Insider Trading

Analysis of Corporate Scandals and Their Impact on the Market

Harshad Mehta, Ketan Parekh, Nirav Modi, the PNB Scam, Kingfisher Airlines and Satyam Computers. We have all heard these names. All of them are associated with negative events or scams. These are the scams which shook the nation and culminated in various changes being made in corporate laws to safeguard ordinary investors. One thing we need to realize is that all these scams could damage public wealth because of the lack of disclosures and bad corporate governance practices. In this section, we will try to understand the core issues in those scams, in order to ensure that these scams do not lead to the destruction of public wealth at large.

Harshad Mehta scam: This is known as the mother of all corporate scams in India. The scam had shaken the entire stock market. Mehta exploited several loopholes in the banking system to carry out his fraudulent activities. He took advantage of the lack of coordination and regulation between banks and the absence of an online trading system. Basically, this scam could be executed because of the lack of regulations. As a regulator, SEBI had very limited authority then. The volume of the scam was worth Rs 4000 crore in 1992, around Rs 22,000 crore as per the current value. Though the scam was a negative development, it had one positive consequence: SEBI was empowered to take action. Since then, SEBI has been monitoring the markets admirably.

Stocks impacted by the Harshad Mehta scam: Although Harshad Mehta operated many smaller stocks, the most important and the largest he manipulated was ACC, his favourite stock. He always quoted the replacement cost theory for the justification of the share price. The theory said that the stock must be valued on the same valuation which is needed to re-establish that company in current time. This action led ACC to get out of hand, going from Rs 200 to Rs 9000, in just three months.

PNB/Nirav Modi scam: The PNB/Nirav Modi scam refers to a major financial fraud that took place in India, involving the Punjab National Bank (PNB) and a diamond jeweller named Nirav Modi. The scam, unearthed in 2018, exploded, affecting the entire PSU banking space in India. Nirav Modi allegedly misguided the banks to the tune of Rs 14,000 crore. He and his uncle, Mehul Choksi, who was the owner of Gitanjali Gems, allegedly engineered the scam with the help of certain PNB officials.

To control the menace of offenders escaping to foreign countries in order to avoid consequences, the Indian government enacted the Fugitive Economic Offenders Act (2018) with effect from 21 April 2018. Under this act, any person who has committed an offence such as counterfeiting government stamps or currency, dishonouring a cheque, money laundering, conducting transactions defrauding creditors and other offences, amounting to Rs 100 crore or more, and has left India to avoid prosecution and refuses to return, can be declared as a fugitive economic offender.

Stock impacted by the Nirav Modi scam: The stock mainly impacted by this scam was PNB, which had to bear the brunt of the loan becoming a non-performing asset (NPA). Though the manipulation was not related to the stock markets directly, it was impacted to a large extent as a large loan had become an NPA.

Satyam Computers: On an ordinary working day in 2009, Satyam Computers' founder wrote a letter, admitting to having inflated the accounts of Satyam Computers with profits of Rs 7000 crore. He confessed that he had been inflating the books for years and that the profits shown in the books had actually never existed. He had even tried to evade the issue by merging Satyam Computers and Maytas Infrastructure (a subsidiary of Satyam) but the effort had failed.

The scam shocked the business world; it was termed the biggest corporate governance failure in India ever. Later, the government superseded the board and finally Satyam Computers was sold to the Mahindra Group. Ramalinga Raju and others involved in the scam were charged with various offences, including cheating, forgery and conspiracy. In April 2015, Raju and nine others were found guilty and sentenced to various prison terms.

The Satyam scandal had shocked regulators, auditors and businesses in India, leading to reforms in corporate governance practices and increased scrutiny of financial reporting and auditing standards. It also highlighted the importance of transparency, ethical practices and accountability in corporate affairs. Some experts termed the Satyam scam as the Indian Enron.

Stock impacted by the Satyam scam: Satyam and Maytas were both impacted by the inflated balance sheet scam of Satyam Computers. The day the scam broke, Satyam's stock went down to around 70 per cent. Finally it was sold to Tech Mahindra and Maytas was sold to IL&FS.

Kingfisher Airlines: This was not just a scam; it was also accompanied by bad business decisions by Vijay Mallya and his family. The Mallya family kept investing in the business even when it was on the verge of closure. There were various allegations of fund diversion. Mallya, the chairman of Kingfisher Airlines, faced legal action from various parties, including banks and investigative agencies. He left India in 2016 but the government is still working on extraditing him.

The Kingfisher Airlines scam highlighted issues related to corporate governance, lending practices and regulatory oversight in India. It also exposed the challenges faced by the aviation industry in the country and prompted reforms in bankruptcy and insolvency laws, as well as stricter scrutiny of loan disbursements and recovery processes.

Stocks impacted by the Vijay Mallya scam: This scam not only impacted Kingfisher Airlines directly but also promoter group entities such as United Breweries and United Spirits. Finally, Mallya had to exit the companies.

Market Efficiency

The Concept of Market Efficiency and Its Application to the Indian Stock Market

I regularly field questions from investors who bought a stock on hearing of some news but discovered later that the stock price stayed the same. Or, on the other hand, that they sold a stock on a certain hypothesis, only to find the stock rising in value after they sold it.

For example, from the middle of 2009 to the end of 2016, Reliance Industries showed a lack of performance, even though the profits almost doubled from around Rs 17,000 crore to Rs 35,000 crore annually. This state of performance for a stock signifies that the market behaviour of a stock is never perfect or rather that the market sometimes does not value a stock fairly because it is not always efficient. This is the concept of market efficiency which describes the extent to which asset prices in financial markets reflect all available information. In an efficient market, it is generally believed that the stock prices will keep reflecting all the information fairly and the price movement will change accordingly.

In reality, markets are never 100 per cent rational or efficient. Most of the time, some good information is ignored and, on the other hand, sometimes incorrect information is treated as a game changer. Until all the market participants understand the relevance of information, intelligent traders will make money and reverse their moves, influencing an anxious investor into a bad trade. There are hundreds of such examples every week. Traders need to understand that there will always be certain anomalies on both the upside and downside; we should be wary of these anomalies.

There are three forms of market efficiency:

Weak form efficiency: This is the first level of market efficiency which treats the stock as per the information available in the open market. In such cases, you will see the stock movements in correlation with announcements done by the company on the stock exchange. Generally, this consists of past information available in the public domain; the stock does not react until any fresh disclosure is made by the company. This form of market efficiency is generally considered ineffective in generating abnormal returns in such markets. Stocks trading on these trends usually give normal market-linked returns. The investor is unable to outperform the markets. The charts also move from information to information and do not show any signs of breakout.

Semi-strong form efficiency: In a semi-strong form efficient market, the information is mixed with some intelligence of analytics. When the information available on a stock is mixed with the analysis of factors like economic scenarios, etc., it turns into a semi-strong form efficiency. This involves analysing financial statements and economic indicators. In these cases, a good fundamental analyst always has an advantage as he can link the public information with the hidden potential of the stock. The stock starts showing some early signs of breakouts even when there is no new information available.

Considering Indian markets, this kind of scenario is seen during the announcement of results and other economic events like RBI policy, inflation data and even the budget announcement. The difference between this and the earlier scenario is that this one contains some prediction about the company's performance and its reflection in the stock prices.

Strong form efficiency: In a strong-form efficient market, asset prices reflect all information, both public and private. In this scenario, the prices rise or fall considering all the public and private information. There is very little scope for making money as some of the traders who have access to some insider information about the company have already traded and gained out of the movement. It is very important to understand here that insider trading is a punishable offence by the law. Unfortunately, the market regulator and forces have been unable to stop trades based on insider information.

The efficiency of any market can vary over time and across different asset classes. As an investor or trader, we must understand that no market is perfect and available without anomalies. Markets are always available with certain money-making opportunities. Still, investors should carefully consider their investment strategies and risk tolerance while dealing with market efficiency and should not consider it as a sole factor for investing or trading.

Empirical Analysis of the Efficiency of the Indian Stock Market

The Indian stock market is one of the largest and most dynamic in the world. Over the past few decades, it has grown at an impressive rate and has become an attractive destination for both domestic and international investors. However, the efficiency of the Indian stock market has been the subject of debates among academics and practitioners alike. Historically, we have seen a lot of incidents where the markets have not been able to reflect the best pricing for every stock. We have seen many stocks which showed signs of moving up but somehow could not because of the efficiency factor. Such incidents prove that the markets always have some more information than is available in the public domain. In certain cases, you will see that few stocks have the best of fundamentals but those will not move in tandem with earnings. The reason is that the market participants have more information than what is available in the public domain. This information could be about the company's financials or even the promoters. On the other hand, there will be a few stocks where the earnings will either remain stable or will deteriorate, but still the stocks will keep flying like a rocket.

One of the best examples of this efficiency are some Adani group stocks. For instance, if we take Adani Enterprises, the company did not do much in terms of earnings from 2019 to 2022, but the stock kept on flying. The details can be seen in the charts below where the first one shows earnings and the second shows price movement.

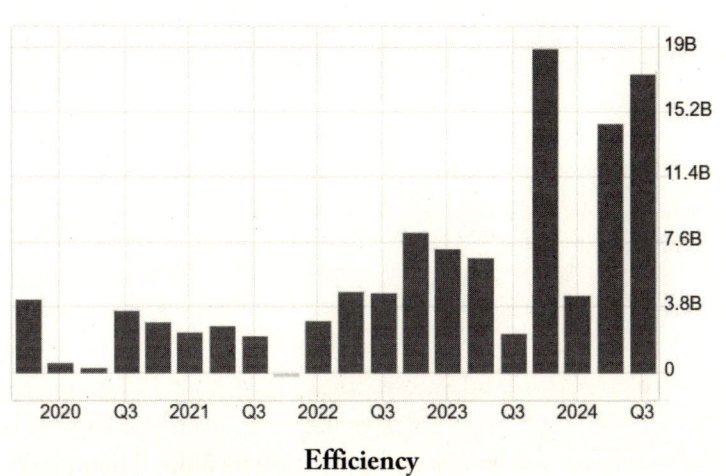

Efficiency

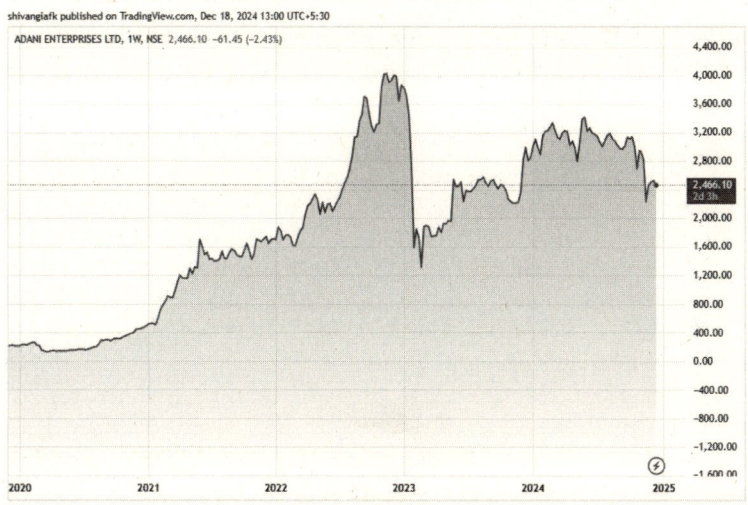

Adani Chart

Here we can clearly see that there is something which is known to market participants. This is a classic case of strong form efficiency where the stock not only reflects public information but also a lot of privately known information.

Part 2

Trading and Investing

Chapter 3

Technical Analysis: Candlestick Patterns, Trading Indicators and Indicator-Based Trading Strategies

Technical analysis: Technical analysis is a method used to evaluate stocks based on their price and volume history. It is a kind of data-based extrapolation of the stock's price which might be in the range of a few minutes to many years. Technical analysts use charts and other tools to identify patterns and trends in stock prices and volumes. Some common technical analysis tools used in the stock market include moving averages, RSI, MACD, etc.

Trading Strategies and Risk Management Techniques

Trading strategies refer to the set of rules and techniques that traders use to identify profitable trading opportunities and to execute trades. Different traders use different trading strategies, which are often based on their individual risk tolerance, investment goals and market analysis. Moreover, trading strategies are trading calls based on market experience; they are used by traders to generate profits from prevalent market conditions. Although there are various techniques in the market, these techniques are ever evolving and newer strategies keep coming to the market.

Some popular trading strategies include:

Trend-following strategy: A trend-following strategy is a trading strategy that involves identifying the direction of the trend in the market and making trades based on that direction. The strategy tracks the price and volume behaviour of the market or stock and extrapolates the next move accordingly. The idea behind this strategy is that markets tend to move in trends, and traders can profit from these trends by buying when the market is in an uptrend and selling when it is in a downtrend.

Techniques of technical analysis are often used for this strategy. The price points are plotted on the chart and the next move of the stock or markets is extrapolated. Traders may use indicators such as moving averages, trend lines or price channels to determine the direction of the trend. Once they have identified the trend, they will then look for opportunities to enter trades in the direction of the trend.

For example, if the market is in an uptrend, the trader may look for opportunities to buy when the price dips to a support level or when a bullish signal is generated by their technical indicators. They may then set a stop-loss order to limit their potential losses if the trend gets reversed. These strategies are used from very short-term time horizons like a single day to even a year.

In the chart below, we can see a clear trend line which tells us about the upward trend of the stock's performance.

Momentum strategy: A momentum strategy is a trading strategy that involves the buying of stocks or other assets that have shown a strong upward momentum and the selling of those that have shown a downward momentum. The idea behind this strategy is that assets that have been performing well are likely to continue to perform well in the near future, while those that have been performing poorly are likely to continue to underperform. The weak ones tend to remain weak for some more time and the strong ones will rule the market.

The best part is that the market gives both opportunities, i.e., buying and selling.

Foreign Investments

Source: www.india-briefing.com

It is important to note that momentum trading can be risky, as there is always the possibility of a sudden reversal in price direction. These reversals can take place due to economic or even political reasons. Any important event in the market can suddenly change the momentum. For example, a change in the interest rates as per RBI policy can change the course of action of a stock or of the entire market. Therefore, traders often use risk management techniques such as stop-loss orders and position sizing to limit their potential losses. Additionally, momentum trading may require frequent monitoring and active management to ensure that positions are exited at the appropriate time.

Contrarian strategy: A contrarian strategy is a trading strategy that involves taking positions that are opposite to the prevailing market sentiment. In short, these are fondly called Contra strategy in the market. This strategy involves buying assets that are currently out of favour with the market and selling those that are popular. It is like taking a risk and floating against the tide.

The idea behind a contrarian strategy is that markets can sometimes overreact to news or events, causing assets to be overbought or oversold. This can create opportunities for contrarian traders who believe that the market sentiment is not justified by the underlying fundamentals of the asset. For example, when the news of the lockdown was announced in 2020, the market suddenly fell but within a few days, it started bucking the trend. The rest is history. To implement a contrarian strategy, a trader will typically look for assets that are currently unpopular or undervalued. To understand the undervaluation, the trader can use any of the valuation techniques which he believes in.

Here, we must understand that taking a contrarian call in the markets is never easy. You need to be very experienced to make it work. You need to understand the market well to use this technique. It is never easy to trade against the trend and a trader must always take a very cautious approach to trade using this strategy.

Value strategy: A value strategy is a trading strategy that talks about the overall valuation of the stock. It works on the belief that most of the stock is either overvalued or undervalued in the market, but that over a period, the markets adjust to the valuation, giving the trader a chance to make money. The overvaluation or undervaluation can be related to the market's perception about growth in the earning of a particular stock.

In order to trade under this strategy, the trader will work on identifying stock which is overvalued or undervalued on a fundamental basis. For example, a trader may look for those stocks which have 15 per cent annual earnings growth but command 70 PE. Those stocks are overvalued and the trader would like to sell/short sell the stock. Practically, we must also understand that value is sometimes about perception or expectation. If we see the Adani group basket of stocks, none of the stocks are cheaper in terms of valuation but even after the fall that followed the Hindenburg report, almost all the stocks scaled back to the highs.

Scalping strategy: A scalping strategy is a short-term trading strategy that involves making multiple trades within a short period of time to take advantage of small price movements in the market. The goal of a scalping strategy is to make small profits on each trade; these can add up to a significant profit over time. Under this strategy, the trader is not looking for larger profits but multiple instances of small-time profits.

The trader will keep looking for those stocks which work in the range but keep making small price movements on either side. In general, defensive stocks like FMCG are the best choice for this category of trade.

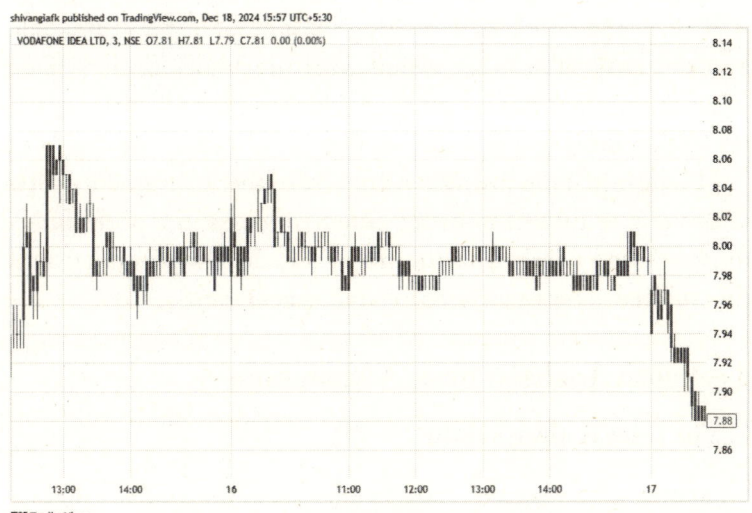

Scalping

If you see the chart displayed above on a regular day, it largely moves in a range. In that case, the trader can't benefit by hoping for a larger swing. Rather, the scalping strategy of making multiple trades within a small range will be helpful.

Risk management techniques are crucial for any trader or investor. The goal of risk management is to reduce the potential losses that can occur during trading or investing. Some popular risk management techniques include:

Stop-loss orders: These are orders that automatically sell a security when it reaches a certain price level, which can help limit losses. Stop-loss should be resorted to frequently as this is the only tool which protects the traders' capital.

Diversification: This involves investing in a variety of different securities in order to spread risk across different asset classes and industries. This reminds us of the old saying, 'Don't put all your eggs in one basket'. At any given time, some sectors may perform well while others may not.

Position sizing: This involves determining the appropriate size of a position based on the amount of capital available and the level of risk associated with the trade. Traders must avoid taking that size of position which is beyond their capital protection limit.

Hedging: This involves using derivative instruments such as options or futures to offset potential losses in a portfolio. It must be used wisely, and the trader should always understand the difference between hedging and speculation.

Technical Analysis: Basic Assumptions

1. The price is always right

This assumption suggests that all relevant information, including past trading data, fundamental factors and market psychology, is already reflected in the price of an asset. Therefore, technical analysts primarily focus on analysing price movements and patterns to make trading decisions. That is why it is often said, '*Bhav bhagwan che*'.

2. The trend is your friend and the price moves in a trend

Technical analysts believe that prices tend to move in upward, downward or sideways trends. Identifying and following these trends is crucial for successful trading. For example, to find the basic trend, we can use a moving average. If the price is above 50 Exponential Moving Average (EMA), it is said to be in the uptrend in the short term.

3. History repeats itself

Another fundamental assumption of technical analysis is that historical price movements tend to repeat in the future. Patterns and behaviours observed in the past are expected to recur under similar market conditions. Traders use this principle to identify recurring patterns and anticipate potential price movements.

4. The price needs confirmation from volumes

Technical analysts consider trading volume as an important confirmation tool for price trends. Increasing trading volume during a price movement is seen as a sign of strength, confirming the validity of the trend. Conversely, decreasing volume may indicate weakness and potential trend reversal.

Technical analysis operates on the premise that market behaviour is largely influenced by human psychology, with 80 per cent of its dynamics being psychological and 20 per cent logical and rational. In contrast, fundamental analysis attributes 80 per cent of market behaviour to logical factors and only

20 per cent to psychology. Nonetheless, both methodologies agree on the legitimacy of current security prices, which reflect the collective wisdom of market participants. By scrutinizing price–volume movements, technical analysis seeks to ascertain the prevailing forces of the supply and demand of financial assets to forecast future prices.

Candlestick Patterns

Candlestick patterns are basically a form of technical analysis used by traders to make decisions about the trend of a stock during a particular period of time. This period can range from a minute to a week and so on. These patterns are formed by the price movements of an asset over a certain period, typically represented by candlesticks on a price chart. Each candlestick provides information about the opening, closing, high and low prices within the chosen time frame. In this section, we will discuss some of the mostly widely used and important types of candlesticks patterns. You can consider candlesticks as a tussle between buyers and sellers. It tells us about the mindset of buyers and sellers and helps us understand how they are reacting and behaving.

Getting the Basics Right

This real body represents the price range between the opening and closing of that day's trading. When the real body is filled in or black (also red), it means that the closing was lower than the opening. If the real body is white (or green), it means that the closing was higher than the opening. The shadows show the high and low prices of that day's trading. If the upper shadow on a down candle is short, it indicates that the opening on that day was near the day's high. A short upper shadow on an up day indicates that the closing was near the high.

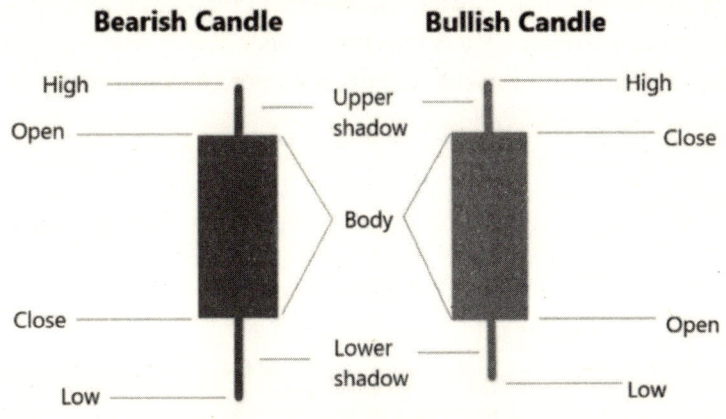

Bullish and Bearish Candle

A Doji: A doji represents an equilibrium between supply and demand. It is a game which is neither in favour of the bulls nor the bear. In the case of an uptrend, as we can see in the below image, the length of each part of the candle is the same which means that first, the bulls ruled the trade and later on the bear charged it or it could be vice versa. Neither buyers nor sellers were able to dominate the candle so the reversal of the earlier trend is possible.

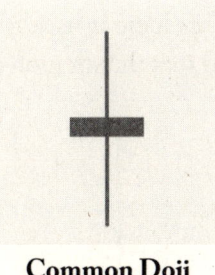

Common Doji

A 'Long-Legged' Doji: Here we can say that the price moved a bit higher but then could not be sustained, then the bear ruled the trade for a longer period of time. We can see that the upper part of the candle is shorter and once the bear started its grip on the trade, it took the lower part for a longer duration. It signified that the prices moved higher but could not be sustained there.

Long-Legged

A 'Gravestone' Doji: This could even be an extension of the candle we studied in the earlier part. It says that the price rose very high in the initial trade but then finally closed at the same level where it had started. It is quite notable that unlike the long-legged doji, the prices here finally settled at the same level and did not go down further. The logic behind this belief is that the buyers were trying to take the stocks up but could not sustain the price and the sellers came back in action. This logic is usually formed in the uptrend and signifies reversal and that the strength of the buyers has ended.

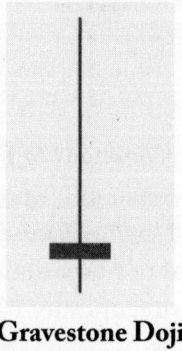

Gravestone Doji

A 'Dragonfly' Doji: A dragonfly doji depicts a period during which prices opened high, sold off and then returned to the opening price. So, technically we saw the bulls in the first part, bears in the second part and finally the bulls in the third part. The logic behind this belief is that the sellers were trying to take the stocks down but could not sustain the prices and the buyers came back in action. This doji is usually formed in the downtrend and signifies reversal and that the strength of the sellers has ended.

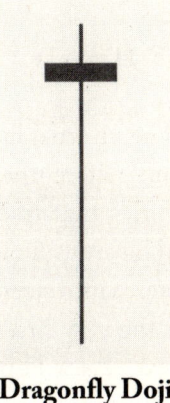

Dragonfly Doji

The Hammer: The hammer and the inverted hammer are only formed in the downtrend and signify reversal. On the day of the hammer candle, there is strong selling, often beginning at the opening bell. As the day goes on, however, the market recovers and closes near the unchanged mark or, in some cases, even higher. In these cases, the market is potentially 'hammering' out a bottom. The logic is that the stock was in the downtrend which means the sellers were dominating. On this candle again, the sellers tried to dominate but could not, and the buyers regained strength and pushed upwards.

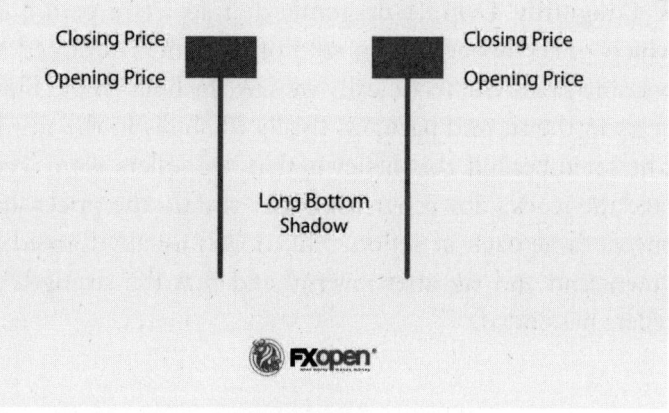

Hammer

The Inverted Hammer: The inverted hammer is the culmination of a sustained downtrend where the stock is already in an oversold scenario. It signifies that traders who have held long positions in the stock and have sustained high losses are joining the race by selling their shares into strength. Here on this candle, sellers dominated but for the very first time, the buyers tried to show some sign of strength. As a Hindi saying goes, '*Himmat ki keemat hai*'. For the first time, buyers showed strength and a willingness to reverse.

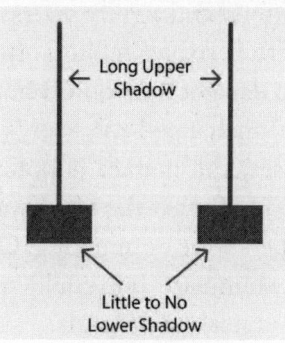

Inverted Hammer

The Shooting Star: Whenever an inverted hammer is made in an uptrend, it is known as a shooting star. A shooting star will, in general, have a small real body and a large upper shadow. Typically, there will either be no lower shadow or a very small one. When such a candle is formed, the markets should ideally gap higher. At first the stocks rally very sharply, but later on, profit taking comes into the picture and then the stock closes nearly unchanged. On the shooting star candle, the buyers tried to dominate but could not and the sellers re-entered the market.

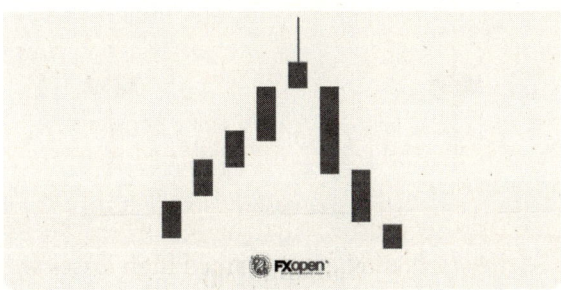

Shooting Star

The Hanging Man Candle: The hammer, when formed in an uptrend, is known as a hanging man. As we can see clearly in the given picture, it is a formation that looks as if someone has been hanged. This generally takes form when there is quite a sell-off in the markets and then the buyers flock in to buy the shares at bargain prices.

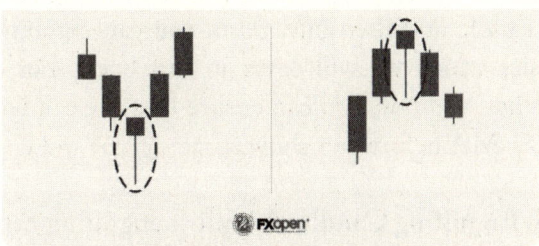

Hanging Man vs Hammer

Spinning Top: A spinning top candlestick pattern is characterized by a small body with upper and lower wicks that are longer than the body itself. It indicates indecision in the market between buyers and sellers. The opening and closing prices are often close to each other, resulting in a small real body. It is a candle which can reverse the trend, if there is an uptrend going on, then the downtrend can start and vice versa.

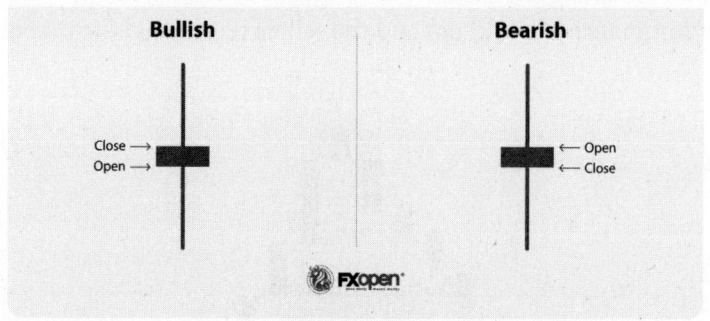

Spinning Top

Important point: All the above were single candlestick patterns. Always remember that working only on candles can be quite misleading—look for price action and patterns for confirmation. Even if you want to work on candles, wait for confirmation and then start. For example, if a downtrend is going on and you suddenly have a hammer, you shouldn't just buy randomly. You should wait for the next candle to break the high of the hammer, keep the stop-loss at the bottom of the hammer candle and then buy. Also, you can combine it with other basics which we will cover in this book. For example, EMA. When you buy, you can ensure that the candle is above 50 or 200 EMA before you show some sign of strength.

A Bullish Engulfing Candle: A bullish engulfing candlestick pattern is a two-candle pattern that typically occurs during a downtrend and signals a potential reversal to the upside.

It can be identified when a small black candlestick, showing a bearish trend, is followed the next day by a large white candlestick, showing a bullish trend. The body of the second candle completely overshadows and engulfs the earlier candle; that is why it is called an engulfing candle. Technically it is a pattern where the bull is in charge, as opposed to the previous day when the bear was in charge.

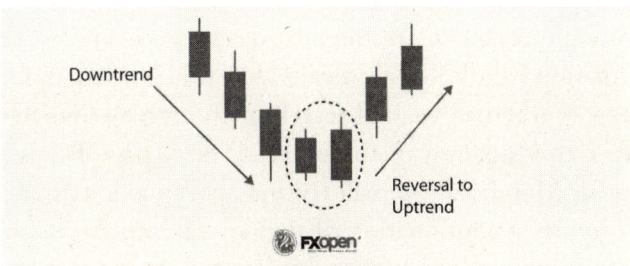

Bullish Engulfing

A Bearish Engulfing Candle: A bearish engulfing candlestick pattern is a two-candle pattern that usually develops during an uptrend and indicates a potential reversal to the downside. It occurs after a significant uptrend. Again, the shadows need not be surrounded. Technically it is opposite the bullish engulfing candle. In a bearish engulfing candle, the bears are in charge of the day, as opposed to the bulls who were in charge on the previous day.

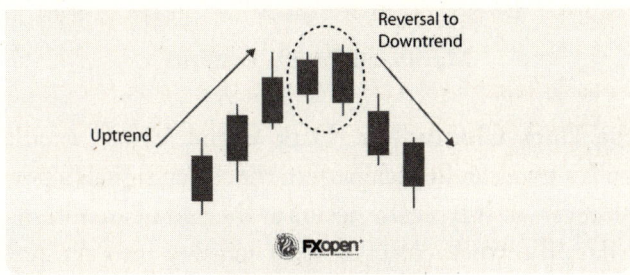

Bearish Engulfing

Marubozu: A Marubozu candlestick is a single-candle pattern that has a very long body with little to no wicks or shadows at the top and bottom. It signifies strong buying or selling pressure throughout the trading period. There are two types of Marubozu candles: bullish and bearish. The one with no wicks is called a full Marubozu candle. If the candle is green or bullish, it means that the buyers are flocking to buy, and vice versa when it is a red or black candle. To validate the trend, it is very important to see the next day's trend. This is a trend confirmation candle which means that if it is a largely bullish or green Marubozu, we will search in an uptrend and this will signify a continuation of the uptrend. Similarly, if it is a red or bearish Marubozu, we will try and spot in a downtrend and it will signify a continuation of the downtrend. An important point to keep in mind is that this pattern should not be used randomly on the index as it can give a lot of fake indications on the index.

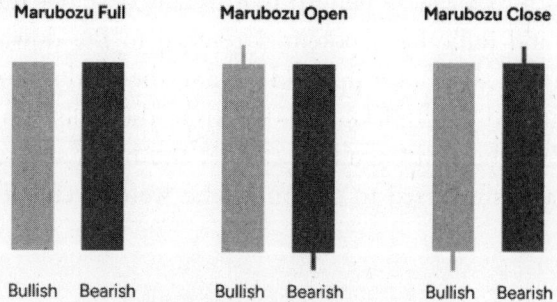

Marubozu Candle Patterns

On the Dark Cloud: The 'Dark Cloud Cover' candlestick pattern is a two-candlestick pattern that often signals a potential bearish reversal. It typically occurs at the end of an uptrend. On cover day, the stock closes at least halfway into the previous white capping candle.

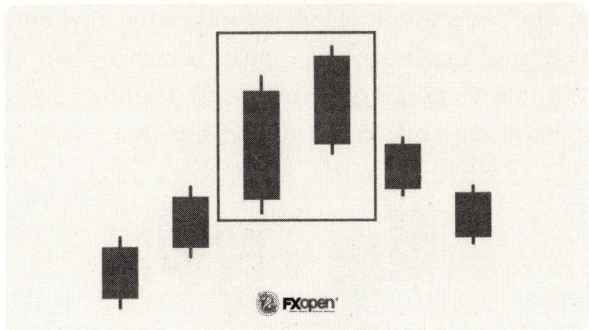

Dark Cloud Cover

A Piercing Pattern: The Piercing Pattern candlestick formation is a bullish reversal signal observed in financial markets. Comprising two candles, it typically emerges after a downtrend. The first candle is bearish, reflecting prevailing selling pressure. However, the second candle opens lower, indicating a continued bearish sentiment. Yet, it closes significantly higher, piercing through the midpoint of the body of the first candle.

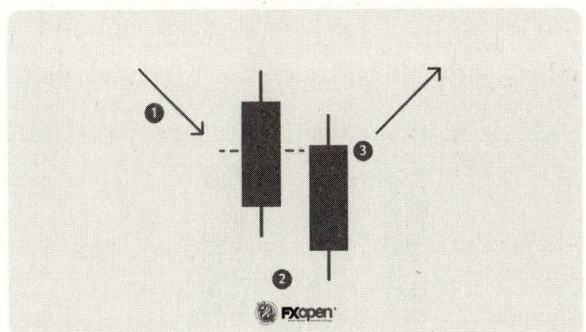

Piercing

The Morning Star: The Morning Star candlestick pattern signifies a bullish reversal. Composed of three candles, it follows a downtrend. The first candle is bearish, followed by a middle day which is not a perfect star, because there is a small lower shadow. The third candle is bullish, indicating a potential shift in momentum from bearish to bullish. Traders often interpret this pattern as a signal to consider long positions or close out shorts, with attention to confirmation signals.

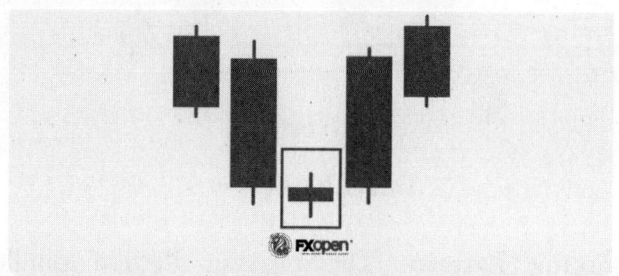

Morning Star

The Evening Star pattern: The Evening Star candlestick pattern signals a bearish reversal in financial markets. Comprising three candles, it follows an uptrend. The first candle is bullish, followed by a small-bodied candle with an upward gap. The third candle is bearish, indicating a potential shift in momentum from bullish to bearish. Traders often interpret this pattern as a signal to consider short positions or close out long positions, with attention to confirmation signals.

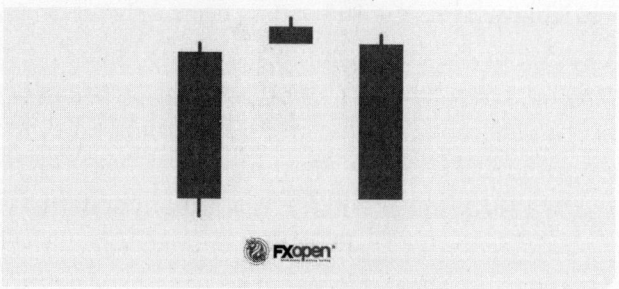

Evening Star

The Bullish and Bearish Harami Candle: The Bullish and Bearish Harami candle can occur in either bullish or bearish trends, but the colours are reversed. A large, black body precedes a smaller, white real body, and this gives out a bullish signal, implying that the stock is poised to move upward. In either bullish or bearish haramis, the upper and lower shadows may be of any size; theoretically they could even go above the real body of the clear candle day. In practice, however, the harami day's shadows are often small and typically well contained within the real body of the previous day's candle.

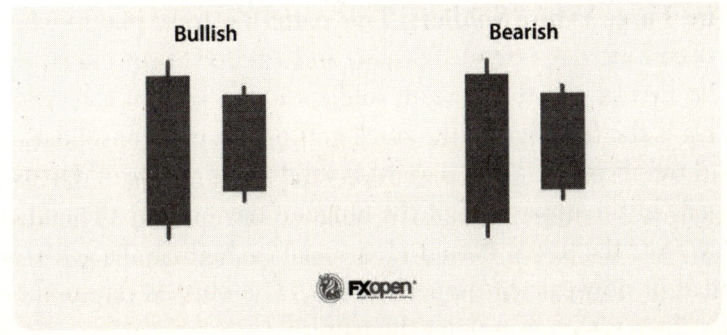

Harami

The Three Black Crows Candle Formation: The Three Black Crows candlestick pattern is a bearish reversal signal in markets. Comprising three consecutive long and bearish candles, it appears after an uptrend. Each candle opens within the previous candle's body and closes lower, forming a downward staircase pattern. This generally continues for three days; that is why it is called Three Black Crow candle pattern. This is largely considered as a signal of a further downside in the stock. Traders either take short calls or cut all open long positions.

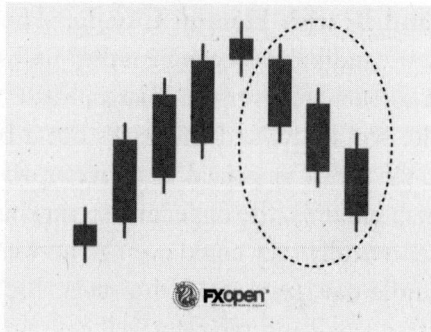

Three Black Crows

The Three White Soldiers: This pattern is most potent when it occurs after an extended decline and a period of consolidation. The first of the three white soldiers is the sign of a reversal. This is the first sign of the stock getting out of a consolidation and trend reversal. The pattern is valid if the candle of day two opens in the upper half of the range of day one. By the end of day two, the stock should close near its high, leaving a very small or non-existent upper shadow. The same is repeated on day three which completes the pattern.

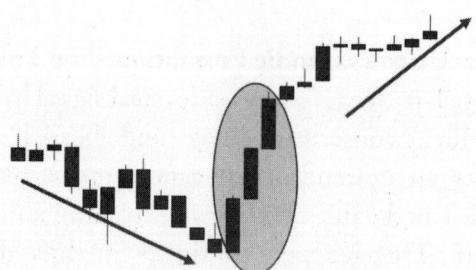

Three White Soldiers

Trading Indicators

Trading indicators are tools used by traders to analyse market data and take informed decisions. These indicators tell the trader about the current set-up of a particular stock or the overall markets. These indicators help identify trends, momentum, volatility, and overbought or oversold conditions. Here we must understand that generally, a single indicator is not of much use unless it is on a strong footing. Rather, multiple indicators are used in combination. In the upcoming section, we will try to understand some of the widely used trading indicators.

Simple Moving Average

The 'simple moving average' (SMA) is an indicator used to identify the direction of a current price trend, without the interference of shorter-term price spikes. The MA indicator combines price points of a financial instrument over a specified time frame and divides it by the number of data points to present a single trend line. This is nothing but a simple statistical calculation of the price level of a particular stock in the entire market.

The outcome of the data used depends on the length of the MA. For example, a 200-day MA requires 200 days of data. A 200-day MA requires fifty days of data and so on. These indicators mostly tell us about the support and resistance of a particular stock or markets. It is quite notable that the interpretation of support and resistance depends upon the current market trend, which could be bullish, bearish or a consolidation.

Simple MA

Exponential Moving Average

On the other hand, the Exponential Moving Average (EMA) is calculated by placing greater weight on the most recent data points. This means that the price level of recent times will have a larger significance on the outcome of the calculation. This is because EMAs react significantly to the most recent price changes. The most popular EMAs are twelve-day and twenty-six-day EMAs for short-term averages, whereas the fifty and 200-day EMAs are used as long-term trend indicators.

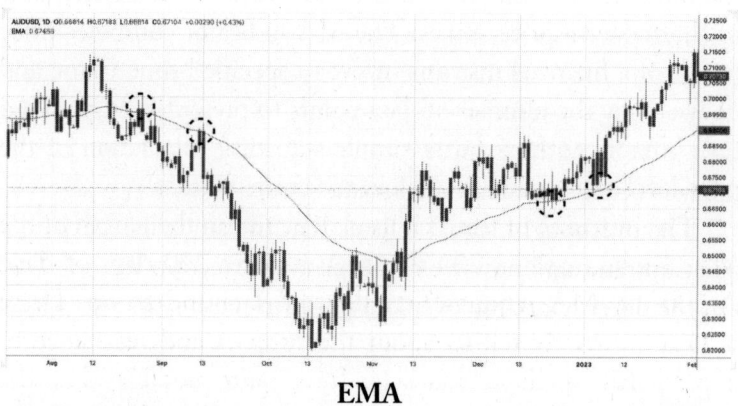

EMA

SMA vs EMA

The terms SMA and EMA are both popular trend-following indicators used in technical analysis. SMA gives equal weight to all the data points within the specified period, providing a smoother line. EMA, on the other hand, gives more weightage to recent data points, making it more responsive to price changes. Traders often use SMA to identify long-term trends and EMA for shorter-term trend analysis and trading signals.

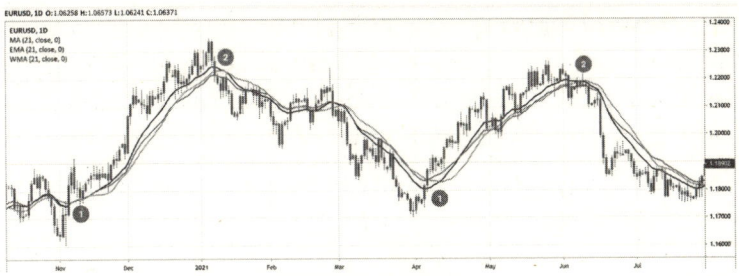

SMA vs EMA

Relative Strength Index

RSI is mostly used to help traders identify momentum, market conditions and warning signals for price movements. It is expressed as a figure between zero and 100. Any stock or index around the seventy level is considered overbought, while near thirty is often considered oversold.

The overbought signal tells us that the stock has been in a quiet uptrend and now we can expect a correction in the price. On the other hand, the oversold position tells us that the stock has faced a lot of bearish momentum and that in the coming days, it could change its position. Here we need to understand that a stand-alone RSI is not the final outcome of a stock's momentum but it has to be seen in conjunction with several other factors.

Overbought Signal: As we have discussed earlier, the RSI indicator is expressed as a value between zero and 100. When the indicator reading approaches the upper end of this range, i.e., above seventy, the stock or index is considered to be overbought. It is a signal that the current movement in the pricing can take a halt and that it is due for a correction. Traders need to be cautious at such times.

Oversold Signal: When the RSI indicator value approaches the lower end of the zero to 100 range, i.e., below thirty, the stock or index in question is considered to be 'oversold'. This is the time when the bearish trend of the stock or the index is about to end and it is ready for some bullish trend and some short-term gains at least.

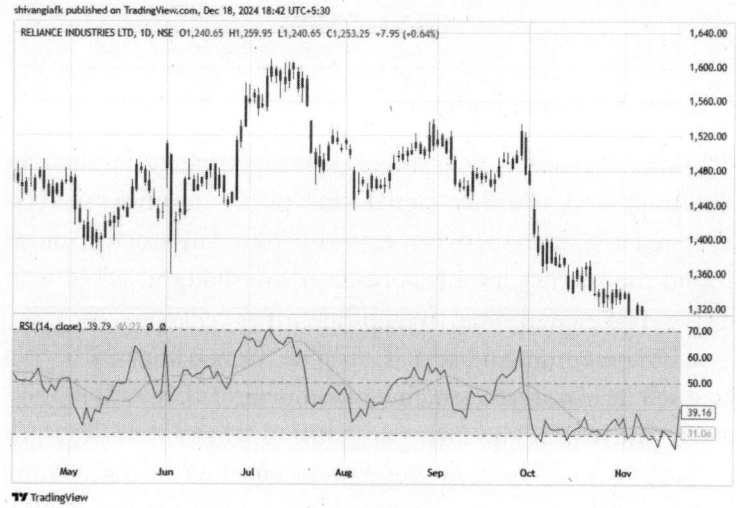

RSI

Moving Average Convergence/Divergence (MACD)

MACD is a widely used momentum indicator in technical analysis. It consists of three components: the MACD line, the signal line and the histogram. The MACD line represents the difference between two exponential moving averages, typically twelve-period and twenty-six-period EMAs. The signal line is a nine-period EMA of the MACD line. Traders use MACD to identify trend direction, momentum shifts, and potential buy or sell signals.

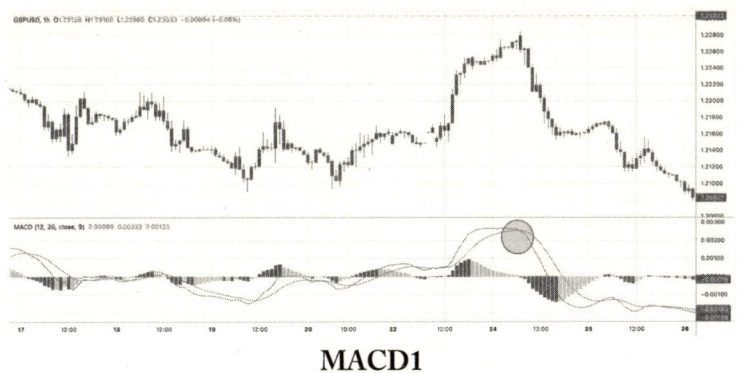

MACD1

The following are the three components of MACD:

-   The MACD line, which measures the distance between two moving averages
-   The signal line, which identifies changes in price momentum and acts as a trigger for buy and sell signals
-   The histogram, which represents the difference between the MACD and the signal line

When calculating the MACD, only two lines are taken into consideration: the MACD line and the signal line. The MACD line is created by subtracting the twenty-six-period moving average from the twelve-period moving average. The signal line is the nine-period moving average of the MACD.

The MACD is then displayed as a histogram, a graphical representation of the distance between the two lines. If the MACD cuts through the signal line from below, traders could use it as a buy signal; if it cuts the signal line from above, traders might use it as a sell signal.

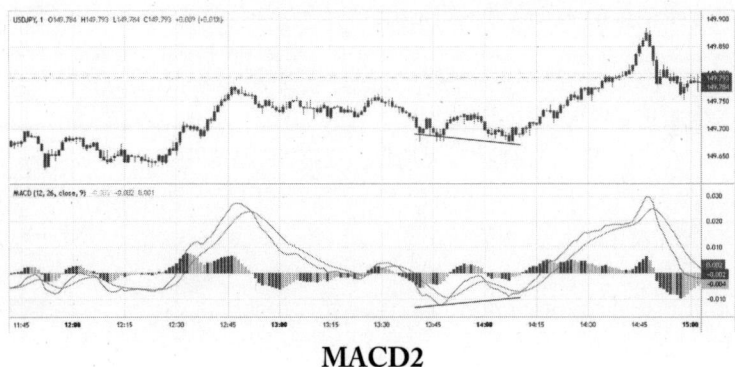

MACD2

ADX Indicator

The Average Directional Index (ADX) is a trend strength indicator used in technical analysis to assess the strength of a market trend, whether it is uptrending or downtrending. ADX measures the strength of a trend, rather than its direction. It ranges from zero to 100, with higher values indicating a stronger trend. Traders typically interpret ADX readings above twenty-five as indicative of a strong trend. Additionally, the ADX can help traders determine whether a market is trending or consolidating. Traders often use ADX in conjunction with other indicators to confirm trends and make more informed trading decisions.

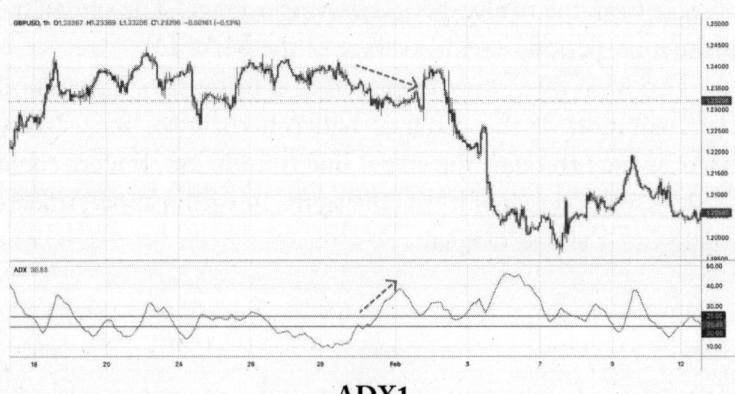

ADX1

Working of ADX Indicator

The ADX indicator derives its strength from its ability to evaluate a trend's magnitude and direction. It accomplishes this by comparing the power of upward price movement (+DI) with the strength of downward price movement (-DI) over a specific period, typically fourteen periods.

The ADX value is calculated using a formula considering both the +DI and -DI values. The formula helps smooth out the data to provide a more accurate representation of trend strength. The resulting ADX value helps traders identify whether a trend is gaining or losing momentum.

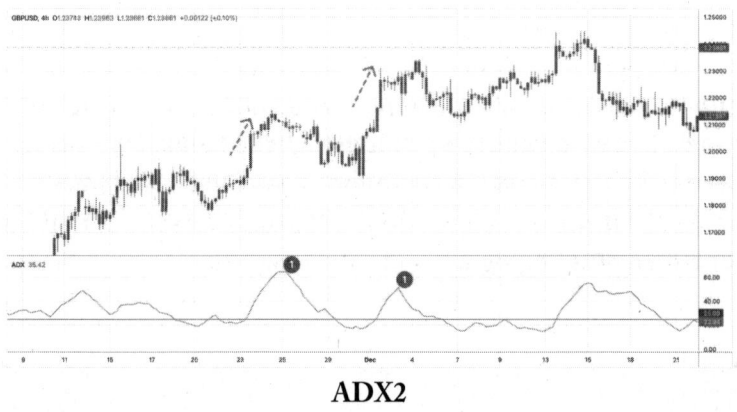

ADX2

Bollinger Bands

Bollinger bands, developed by John Bollinger, are a widely used technical analysis tool. They consist of three lines: a simple moving average (typically twenty periods) and upper and lower bands plotted two standard deviations away from the moving average. These bands dynamically expand and contract, based on market volatility. Traders use Bollinger bands to identify overbought and oversold conditions, potential trend reversals and volatility breakouts. When prices touch or penetrate the bands, it may indicate potential trading opportunities. However, the bands should be used alongside other indicators for comprehensive market analysis and risk management.

How Do Bollinger Bands Work?

Bollinger bands work by providing a visual representation of volatility and potential price levels in financial markets. The bands consist of a moving average line, typically calculated over twenty periods, flanked by upper and lower bands plotted two standard deviations away from the average. These bands get dynamically adjusted according to market volatility, widening during periods of high volatility and narrowing during calmer phases. Traders observe price movements in relation to the bands: touching or penetrating the bands may suggest overbought or oversold conditions, potential trend reversals or breakout opportunities. Bollinger bands serve as a tool for identifying trading signals and managing risk.

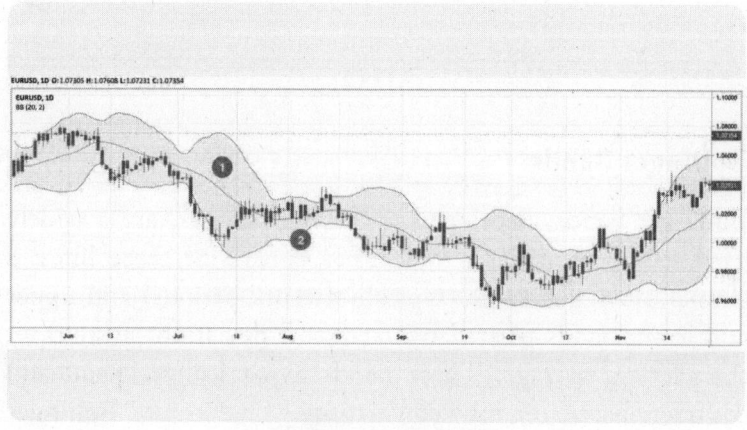

Bollinger Bands

Stochastic Oscillator

The stochastic oscillator, developed by George C. Lane, is a momentum indicator used in technical analysis to measure the relative position of a closing price within a price range over a specified period. It ranges from zero to 100, indicating overbought conditions near 100 and oversold conditions near zero.

A stochastic oscillator is an indicator that compares a specific closing price of an asset to a range of its prices over time—showing momentum and trend strength. A reading below twenty generally represents an oversold market and a reading above eighty an overbought market. However, if a strong trend is present, a correction or rally will not necessarily ensue.

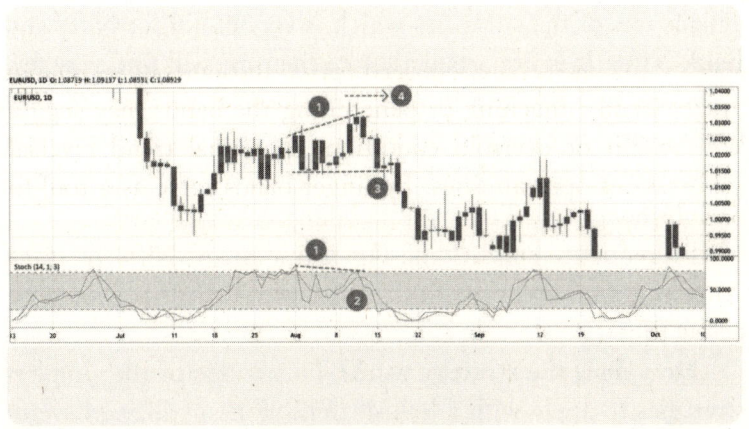

Stochastic Oscillator

Indicator-Based Trading Strategies

RSI-Based Trading Strategies

Relative Strength Index (RSI)

RSI is mostly used to help traders identify momentum, market conditions and warning signals for price movements. RSI is expressed as a figure between zero and 100. Any stock or index around the seventy level is considered overbought, while any stock or index near thirty is often considered oversold. Figures of seventy and thirty are broadly used but for our strategy, we will be changing it a bit.

The overbought signal tells us that the stock has been in a quiet uptrend and now we can expect a correction in the price; on the other hand, the oversold position tells us that the stock has faced a lot of bearish momentum and that in the coming days, it can turn its position. Here we need to understand that stand-alone RSI is not the final outcome of a stock's momentum but it has to be seen in conjunction with a lot of other factors.

Strategy One on RSI

This is one of the strategies which is very useful for Nifty and Bank Nifty. It is important to note that one will find very few occasions to apply this strategy, no more than three to four times a year, but even so it can generate very good returns and carries a very high probability of success. This is basically a buy or bullish strategy. There are no selling positions here.

Prerequisite conditions: For this strategy, Nifty or Bank Nifty must be above its 200 DMA and RSI (10) should be below thirty.

How does the strategy work? This is one of the simplest strategies to apply with a bullish trend. First of all, we have to set RSI (10) and then we have to look at the entry point where RSI is below thirty, which becomes our entry point. Here, we don't need any upper band for RSI as we are not looking for a bearish strategy.

The index must be above 200 DMA; if it goes below 200 DMA, the trend would be considered bearish. In such a trend, it would not be advisable to apply a bullish pattern strategy. Even if the condition of RSI around thirty is being fulfilled, we must apply this only when the index is above 200 DMA. As soon as all the required conditions are met, it will become our entry point. As soon as the RSI goes below thirty and comes back above thirty by undercutting it, that zone becomes our buy point.

Exit Point: Initially the trade should be taken for four to five days and we should exit the trade when the RSI reaches fifty. And even if we want to continue the trade, one may do so for seven days, with a particular stop-loss like recent swing lows or trend line. The stop-loss here is very subjective as the trader should look at the chart where he can find some good support. Else, we can keep the trailing stop-loss at 0.75 per cent of the trade value.

Trading Beyond Indices: This strategy is suitable mostly for Nifty and Bank Nifty, but we will not find regular trades under this. Generally we might find four to five trades in a year. To avoid this problem, we can trade in some of the most liquid stock or mostly frontliners like stocks under Nifty Fifty. Traders are advised not to trade in options in initial trades.

RSI1

RSI2

Strategy Two

Intra-day Trades Under RSI: With certain basic conditions, this strategy can also be applied in intra-day trading but we need to take care of the following aspects:

- The intra-day time frame must be from five to fifteen minutes. Any trade with a shorter duration is not useful.
- The trade must be taken in Nifty or Bank Nifty only.
- The trader should not take more than four trades in a day.
- In case you plan to do more than three trades, your capital must be 50 per cent, in keeping with the capita management rule.

The Intra-day Strategy: While trading intra-day, we will opt for both buy and sell trades. That is why we will need the upper and lower ranges of RSI. Here, we will take the range of seventy-five to twenty-five. When the RSI is above seventy-five, it indicates that the stock has been overbought. When the RSI is below twenty-five, it indicates that the stock has been oversold. In general, we find very few trades in this range so we can set a range of seventy to thirty, where above seventy is overbought and below twenty-five is oversold.

Here, we will be able to see the pattern of W or M too. If it can be combined with your RSI range, you can trade. For example, sometimes the markets will open negative by 300–400 points, then buying will emerge, and then markets will fall again, creating a W pattern. At this point we cannot predict if there will be a breakout or not, but if the index satisfies your RSI conditions, you may go ahead with the trade.

W and M pattern for beginners:

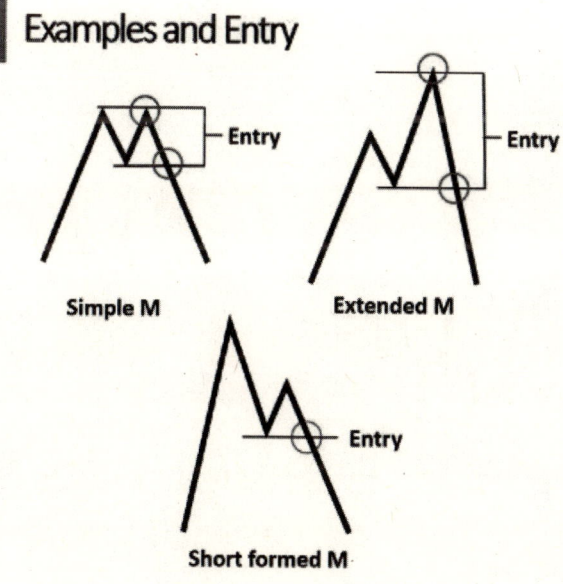

Examples and Entry

Simple M

Extended M

Short formed M

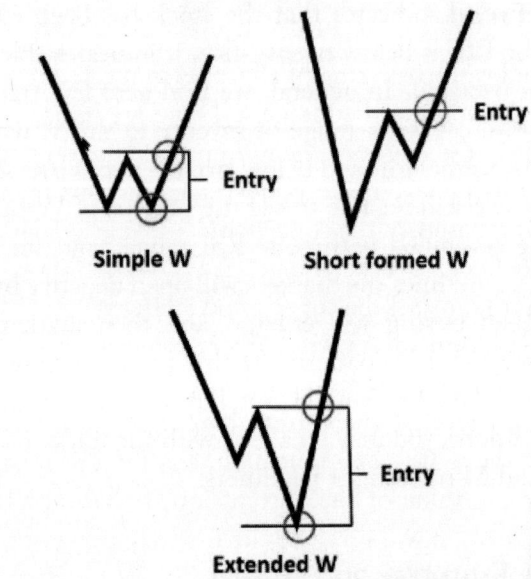

Simple W   **Short formed W**

Extended W

Example:

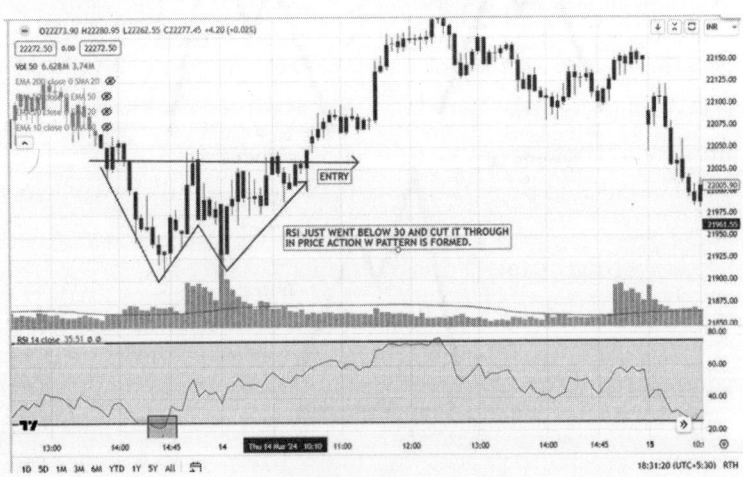

Double Bottom

Super Trend

The trend is the true king of all trades as it can defy most of the other indicator-based strategies. There are basically two types of trends in the markets: the uptrend and the downtrend. This basically helps you make good trades in your own set-up of trades. It is based on the concept of a moving average combined with the Average True Range (ATR). The following are the important points of the super trend strategy:

Calculation of ATR: ATR is calculated as the average of the true ranges over a specified period. The True Range is the highest level of the current high, less the current low; the absolute value of the current high, less the previous close, and the absolute value of the current low, less the previous close. This calculation will give you the first requirement of the super trend strategy.

Once you have the ATR, you can calculate the upper and lower bands of the super trend indicator. The upper band is calculated by adding the product of the ATR and a multiplier which is generally between one and three the moving average. The lower band is calculated by subtracting the product of the ATR and the same multiplier from the moving average.

The calculation of the super trend indicator is shown below:

Up = (high + low) / 2 + multiplier x ATR
Down = (high + low) / 2 - multiplier x ATR

Identifying Trends: Basically, it is a buy signal if the stock crosses the upper band, as per the above calculation, and a sell signal if the stock crosses the lower band. If the super trend indicator moves below the closing price, the indicator turns green, indicating a buy point in the stock. On the other hand, if the super trend closes above, the indicator is in the red zone and it is a sell signal.

Stop-loss: For a long position, you can put the stop-loss right at the green indicator line. For a short position, you can put it at the red indicator line.

Stop-loss

Additional trick: The super trend, as an indicator, often gives fake signals. To reduce the incidence of fake signals, you should approach it with a 50 EMA line. If your chart on the weekly time frame is above 50 EMA, only consider buying set-ups, and if it is below 50 EMA on the weekly time frame, only consider selling set-ups. This might sound simple but it will highly increase the efficiency of your working and success rate.

MACD-Based Trading Strategies

MACD is a widely used momentum indicator in technical analysis. It consists of three components: the MACD line, the signal line and the histogram. The MACD line represents the difference between two exponential moving averages, typically twelve-period and twenty-six-period EMAs. The signal line is a nine-period EMA of the MACD line. Traders use MACD to identify trend direction, momentum shifts, and potential buy or sell signals.

The Strategy: This strategy should not be used on a stand-alone basis. Most of the time, it is used with a super trend or with 'WVAP'. There are basically two components to this. One is the MACD line and the other is the signal line. When the MACD line undercuts the signal line from below, it becomes a buy signal, which is basically a crossover. Another important part of this strategy is that just like the super trend strategy, it carries a 50 per cent chance of turning out right. Our strategy says:

1. For buying: The MACD line cuts the signal line from below. Additionally, the super trend is also indicating Buy (green).
2. For selling: The MACD line cuts the signal line from above. Additionally, the super trend is also indicating Sell (red).

On the other hand, if the MACD line cuts this signal line from above, it becomes a sell signal.

Important points to note:

1. For the Buy signal, the crossover had better be slightly above the zero line. This means that the price is in an uptrend. It will be difficult but will give us double surety.
2. A histogram is also a very significant part of this strategy; it is basically the gap between the MACD and signal line. If the red bar in the histogram goes lower, it means that it is time to buy as a crossover is about to take place.

3. It is important to track the divergence in the histogram and crossover together as there are higher chances of the strategy playing out well. Generally, divergence in the histogram will signal in advance.

The best part about this strategy is that it can be used as a swing or even as an intra-day strategy.

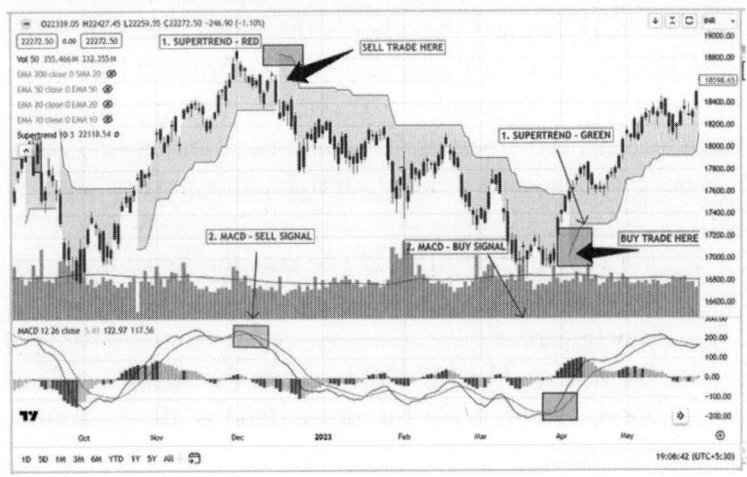

MACD

Bollinger Bands

Bollinger bands, developed by John Bollinger, are a widely used technical analysis tool. They consist of three lines: a simple moving average (typically twenty periods) and upper and lower bands plotted two standard deviations away from the moving average. These bands dynamically expand and contract based on market volatility. Traders use Bollinger bands to identify overbought and oversold conditions, potential trend reversals and volatility breakouts. When prices touch or penetrate the bands, it may indicate potential trading opportunities.

However, they should be used alongside other indicators for comprehensive market analysis and risk management.

Strategy One: First, we have set the line of twenty DMA and two standard deviations on either side. So now we have to understand that there will be a period of consolidation before the period of expansion or contraction, which means that a stock for a particular time frame will not move in a single direction. Before expanding or contracting, it will be in a consolidation phase for some time.

Squeeze: All three lines are set at twenty DMA and two standard deviations on either side are coming very close together or are technically squeezed. Whenever there is a breakout or a breakdown with a large candle, it indicates an entry point for the stock. Here we must keep a risk to reward ratio of 1:3. It is generally seen that this kind of squeeze is formed after the markets have seen recent corrections or a big rally. The exit will depend on your trailing stop-loss strategy. If you have made 20 per cent profit, sell 50 per cent of the quantity and the remaining 50 per cent can be trailed with twenty EMA stop loss.

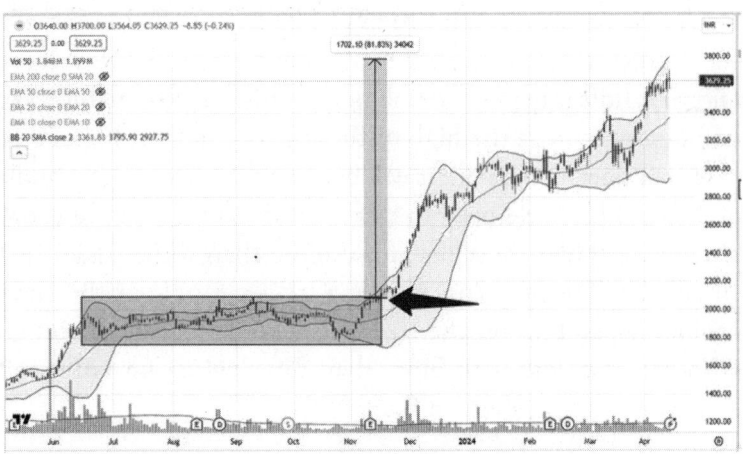

Bollinger 1

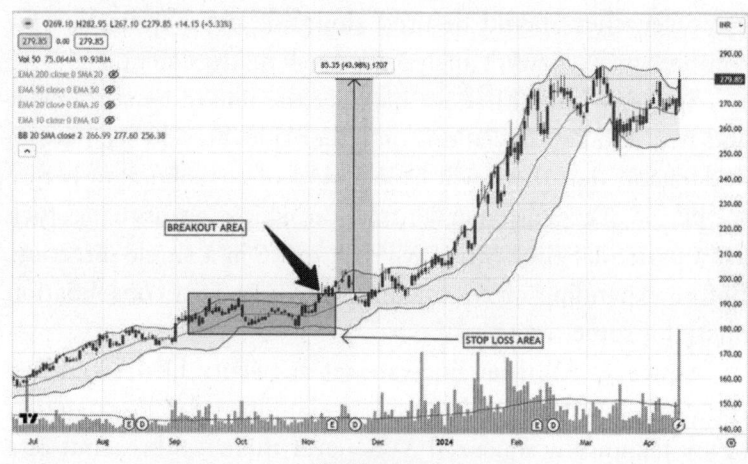

Bollinger 2

Intra-day Strategy/Option Selling: This is basically an option selling strategy. Here we will take a time frame of five minutes and place standard deviations of 1.5 on either side. Now we will look for some candles on either side of the Bollinger band. This will be called a trigger candle. Now if the trigger candle is above the Bollinger bands, we want to short sell, and if it is below the bands, we want to buy. The logic is that eventually the candles should come inside the Bollinger bands. Now if the trigger candle is below the Bollinger bands, we want to buy. We will buy as soon as the high of the trigger candle is broken. In case that doesn't happen, it will become the next trigger candle and so on. Here we need to take note that as it is an intra-day strategy, a trader must not make more than three trades in a single day. The stop-loss can be a trigger candle or the entry candle, depending on the size of the stop-loss. But don't go with the stop-loss with more than forty points on Nifty and seventy to eighty points in Bank Nifty.

Intra-day Strategy

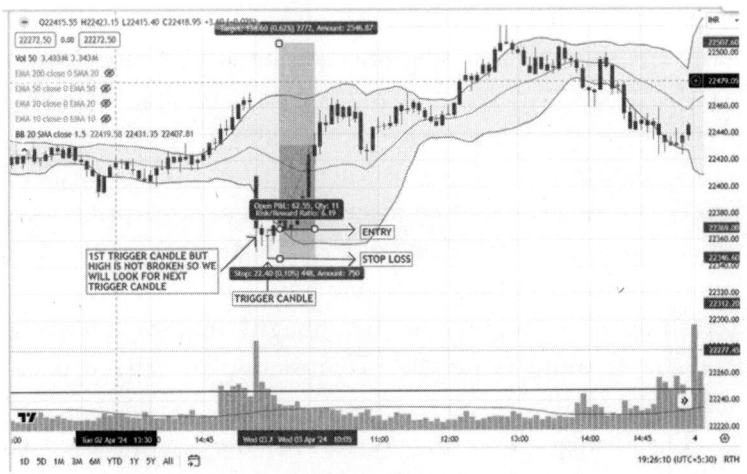

Intra-day 2

Swing Trading in Stocks: Here also we will take 1.5 standard deviations. The important thing here is that we must see the double bottom formation within the Bollinger band. The second bottom formation must be within the band. If it goes below the band, it means that the stock might still be in a downtrend. If the formation is inside the band, it indicates that the stock is trying to make some move up. Stop-loss should be within the low of the swing or 3 per cent of your buying price.

Intra-day Strategy/Option Buying: With the width of the Bollinger band, we can assess the level of contraction and expansion. After a long period of contraction, when the width of the band increases, that becomes an entry point for the stock. The time frame should not be less than fifteen minutes; it could be thirty minutes. So basically, we have to buy the expansion of the index or stock.

Stochastic Oscillator

The stochastic oscillator, developed by George C. Lane, is a momentum indicator used in technical analysis to measure the relative position of a closing price within a price range over a specified period. It ranges from zero to 100, indicating overbought conditions near 100 and oversold conditions near zero.

A stochastic oscillator is an indicator that compares a specific closing price of an asset to a range of its prices over time, showing momentum and trend strength. A reading below twenty generally represents an oversold market and a reading above eighty an overbought market. However, if a strong trend is present, a correction or rally will not necessarily ensue.

The Strategy: This strategy works on the potential oversold and overbought zone and tells us about the price movement of the range of stocks. If we talk about slow stochastic, it tells us about fourteen days' range of the stock of high and low. It is very important to take a call only when you see strong price action at the high and low zones. Sometimes, the traders are trapped as they ignore the trend. First, we must identify the long-term range to make the right trades.

For example, if the stock has a range of fifty to 100 within forty days and it is trading at ninety right now, then we must first identify how far we are from the bottom of that range. So if we are at ninety, we are at Rs 40 or 80 per cent above the bottom of the range. So here in this scale if we are above eighty, we should consider it as overbought, and if it is below twenty, we should consider it oversold. Remember, it is just an indication. If it goes below twenty, we should wait for it to come back by undercutting the chart.

Level One of Strategy: We must identify the long-term trend. We must plot the chart on fifty EMA. If the chart is above fifty EMA, we will only do buy trades, and if the chart is below fifty EMA, we will only do sell trades.

Level Two of Strategy: Now we must apply the strategy on the daily time frame. Now if the slow stochastic is below twenty and is coming back by cutting through the chart, then we have to buy the stock. On the other hand, if it is above eighty, and coming back by uppercutting the chart, we have to sell the stock.

Stop-loss

- The first level of stop-loss can be a generic 3 per cent loss from your price on either side.
- The second level of stop-loss can be the swing lows of the last few days where you see that the stock has taken some support.
- We are at the third level when the slow stochastic chart has gone below twenty.

Important point: All stocks don't work in a fourteen-days' swing. For example, Reliance completes its swing in twenty-five days. So you need to check the swing range of every stock at a specific level.

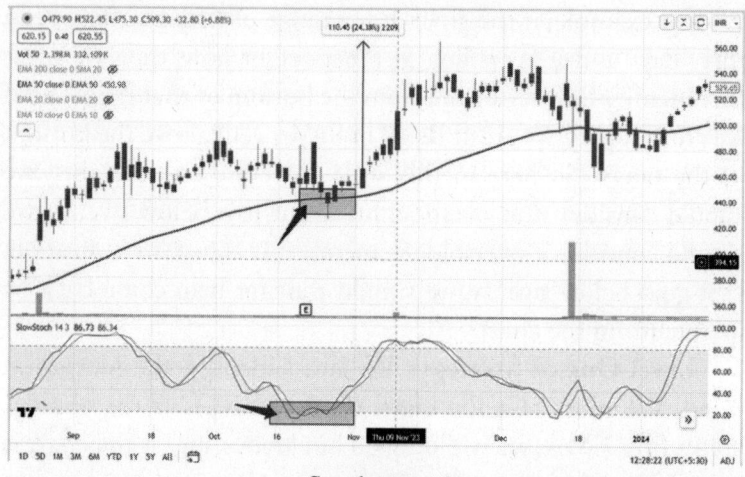

Stochastic 1

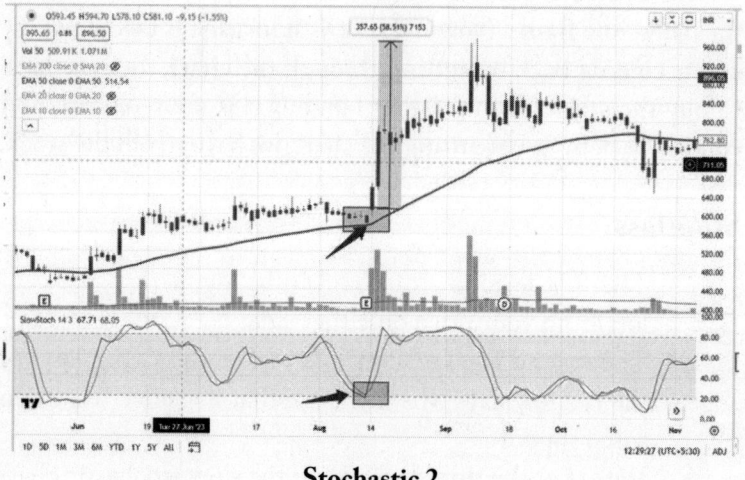

Stochastic 2

Pivot Points

In stock trading, a pivot point is important to gauge the support and resistance point in trading. Computed from the previous day's high, low and closing prices, the pivot point itself represents the average of these values. Surrounding this central pivot are support and resistance levels, calculated based on specific formulas. Basically, pivot points are calculated by taking in mind Resistance One and Resistance Two and Support One and Support Two. They basically tell us the level where the stock can consolidate itself or take a reversal. These pivot points tell the trader about the entry and exit points in a stock.

The basic formula to calculate the pivot point is High+Low+Close/3. In this formula, we will consider the pricing of the previous day.

The Strategy: When we use the 'Pivot Point Standard', it will give us automated points of support and resistance as pivot points calculated on earlier price movements. Basically, the pivot gives us the level from where the stock can bounce. For example, if we see a stock getting resistance on R1 again and again, we will see if it is going down to the pivot. On the other hand, if the stock is crossing R1, then we will see R2 and further resistance. Since the markets are opening above the pivot points on a given day, we can consider that the scenario is bullish, and it can cross resistance with strong momentum.

On the other hand, if the stock takes a turn from resistance and even breaks the pivot point, we need to see if the stock is reaching S1 and S2 and further levels. So, basically the pivot tells us a lot about resistance and support levels.

How to Trade: Pivot is an indictor which follows a particular level and does not change itself as per the pricing on your time frame. It basically tells you about some stagnant levels which play important levels of Resistance and Support. Do not become bearish in a trade until the markets have crossed S1 and S2. If the market goes beyond those levels, it's time to change the view. If the market crosses R1 and R2, it is a good time to be bullish.

Stages of Any Stock

Stocks pass through four stages.

1. **Stage One—The stage at which no one cares**

   During Stage One, a company's earnings, sales and margins are not showing strength, neither is the stock price.

   There is no certainty about the future of the company or sector. Nothing tangible is happening in the stock and it is just consolidating in a range without any significant price increase. One may be tempted to buy the stock based on analyst belief or management commentary or a tip from a random person who doesn't care about your money, but as an informed investor, one must always wait. Not every stock will move to stage Two. It is best to avoid such stocks, if you want to increase your success ratio. During Stage One, the stock price will move sideways with a lack of any sustained price movement up or down. The price may hover around 200 EMA and appear to be stuck in a range. Usually this stage comes after Stage Four where the stock has significantly fallen and cracked. No stock is a good stock until it goes up in price. My purpose is not to buy a stock at the cheapest price available; my purpose is to buy the stock at the right price at the right time where it has the highest potential of giving returns.

2. **Stage Two—Breakout and move stage**

   The very basic nature of this stage is when the daily and weekly price and volume chart will show big up candles, representing large volumes on rallies, and even if there are pullbacks, they are slow and on low volumes. Here is some simple price action to spot this stage: Stock price above fifty days (ten weeks) and the 200 days (forty weeks) moving average, the fifty-day moving average is above the 200-day moving average and the 200-day moving average line is trending up for at least one month.

3. **Stage Three—Exit stage**

It is said that nothing is permanent, so is the movement in any stock. At some point, earnings, though still increasing, are going to rise by a smaller percentage. The stock price may still be moving upwards but it may be experiencing more high-volume pullbacks and increasing volatility. At some point, there will usually be a major price break in the stock on an increase in volume. Often it is the largest one-day decline since the beginning of the Stage Two advance. On a weekly chart, the stock might put in the largest weekly decline since the beginning of the move. These price changes almost always occur on overwhelming volumes and indicate heavy institutional selling.

4. **Stage Four—Falling Knife stage**

As EPS momentum and sales momentum slow down, the stock starts falling. The Stage Four selling may continue for an extended period until it is finally exhausted, and the stock enters another period of ignorance. Features may include the stock breaking the 50 EMA line with volume, 200 EMA line sloping downwards, the stock having more down days than up days, and down days coming with volumes.

It is not necessary that the stock must move from Stage Three to Stage Four. It could move from Stage Three to Stage One again. That would be known as the second breakout. Usually, we can trade up to three breakouts or three bases, but after that, the risk–reward ratio is unfavourable and chances of breakout failure increase to a great extent.

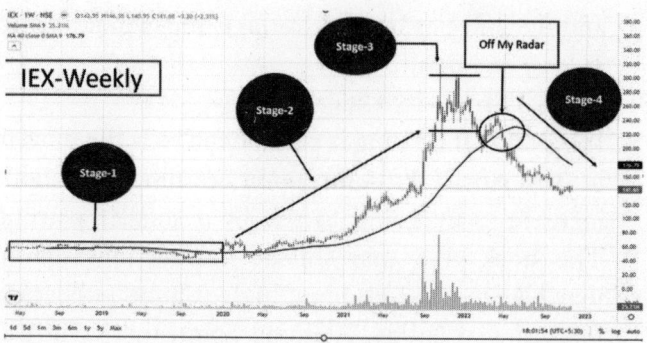

Here we can see big volumes as the price falls denoting a expected reversal typically denoting that the stock has entered into stage-4.

Stage Four 1

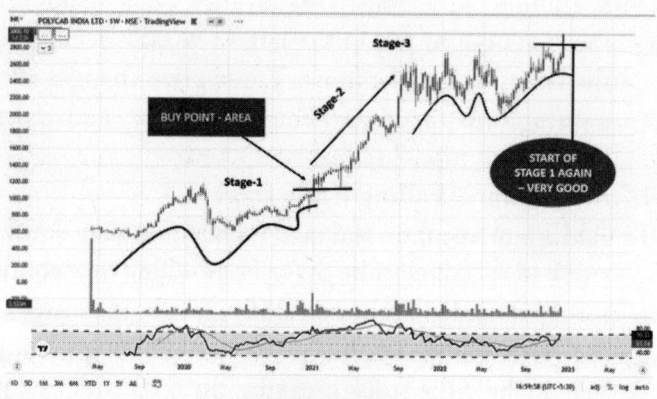

Stage Four 2

Stage Four 3

Chapter 4

Equity Valuation Models and Technical Analysis

Equity valuation models and technical analysis are two common methods used to analyse and evaluate stocks. In this section, we will discuss these methods in brief and try to understand the basics behind these.

Equity Valuation Models: Equity valuation models are used to estimate the intrinsic value of a stock. Intrinsic value refers to the true value of a stock based on its fundamentals, such as earnings, revenue and assets. There are several equity valuation models used by analysts; every model gives a different value of a particular stock. These methods are used by those investors who want to invest money for the long term.

Discounted Cash Flow (DCF) Model: The DCF model is one of the most used methods of stock valuation. It estimates the intrinsic value of a stock by discounting its future cash flows to their present value. This method looks at the current value of the future earning of the campus. This model assumes that the value of a stock is equal to the sum of its future cash flows discounted to their present value. The current interest rate is one of the key factors while using this method of valuation. In other words, the model tells us the current value of Rs 100 earned after ten years if the interest rate is X per cent. Based on that value, the investor will decide to put the money in a certain stock.

The DCF Model involves the following steps:

Forecasting Future Cash Flows: The first step in the DCF Model is to forecast or estimate the future cash flows of the company, analysing the company's financial statements, such as income statements, balance sheets and cash flow statements, to estimate the cash flows that the company is expected to generate in the future. We look at the assessment of the future earning of the company. While doing this, we must remember that these numbers are largely based on extrapolation and assessment and that there can be a margin of error. The following is an example of the assessment of the future cash flow of Adani Ports.

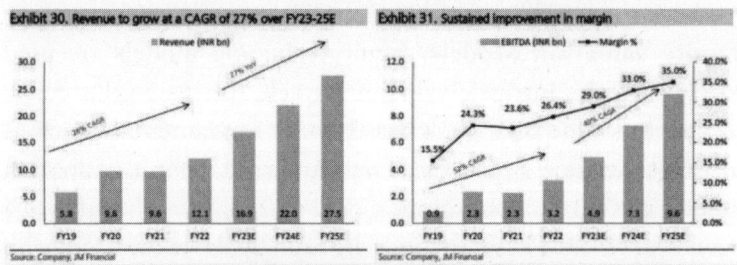

Equity Valuation Model

Determining the Discount Rate: The second step is to determine the discount rate, which is the rate used to discount the future cash flows to their present value. The discount rate is typically based on the risk-free rate of return, plus a risk premium based on the company's level of risk. It tells us how much return the company would have generated, if it had the money. If we park our money in a risk-free fixed deposit at 6 per cent, we can say that the discount rate can be 6+2 per cent.

Discounting Future Cash Flows: The third step is to discount the future cash flows to their present value using the discount rate. This involves dividing the future cash flows by the discount rate raised to the power of the number of years in the future.

Calculating Terminal Value: The fourth step is to calculate the terminal value, which is the estimated value of the company at the end of the forecast period. This is typically calculated using the perpetuity growth method or the exit multiple method.

Calculating Intrinsic Value: The final step is to sum up the discounted future cash flows and the terminal value to arrive at the intrinsic value of the stock.

The formula for the DCF Model can be written as follows:

$$DCF = (CF1 / (1 + r)^{\wedge}1) + (CF2 / (1 + r)^{\wedge}2) + ... + (CFn / (1 + r)^{\wedge}n) + (TV / (1 + r)^{\wedge}n)$$

Where:
DCF: Intrinsic value of the stock
CF1, CF2, . . ., CFn: Cash flows in each year of the forecast period
TV: Terminal value at the end of the forecast period
r: Discount rate or the cost of equity
n: Number of years in the forecast period

The cash flows (CF) in each year are usually calculated as operating cash flows, which are the cash flows generated from the company's operations, minus capital expenditures (CAPEX), which are the investments made in the company's assets. The terminal value (TV) is the estimated value of the company at the end of the forecast period, and it is calculated using either the perpetuity growth method or the exit multiple method.

The discount rate (r) is the rate used to discount the future cash flows and terminal value to their present value. It is usually the cost of equity, which is the return that investors require for investing in the stock of a particular company. The cost of equity can be calculated using the Capital Asset Pricing Model (CAPM), which considers the risk-free rate, the market risk premium and the beta of the company.

The DCF Model is an equity valuation model that is widely used in stock markets because it provides a comprehensive analysis of a company's future cash flows and allows for adjustments to be made for different levels of risk. Even after being one of the most used methods, it is also now almost flawless. The biggest problem faced while using this method is that of extrapolating the cash flows, which is a very difficult number to guess, as the business environment keeps changing, affecting the overall cash flows of the company.

Price to Earnings (P/E) Ratio Model: The Price to Earnings (P/E) Ratio Model is another commonly used equity valuation model in the Indian stock market. It estimates the intrinsic value of a stock by comparing its market price to its earnings per share (EPS). The P/E Ratio is calculated as the market price per share divided by the EPS. There are no complex mathematical calculations involved. The calculation for this valuation is quite easy, but the analysis is important. For example, if we want to calculate the P/E ratio of Ultratech, we must divide the price by the EPS. The price of the share while writing this piece is around 7650 and the EPS of the last twelve months is Rs 175. The P/E ratio of the stock will be 7650/175, i.e., 43.

To understand the P/E ratio concept, we need to understand the point of the trailing P/E and forward-looking P/E. The former concept calculates the P/E based on the declared earning and in the next method, we calculate the P/E based on future projection of earnings.

The P/E Ratio Model analysis involves the following steps:

Calculation of the P/E Ratio: The first step is to calculate the P/E Ratio by dividing the market price per share by the earnings per share (EPS).

Comparison with Industry and Historical Averages: The second step is to compare the calculated P/E Ratio with the industry average and the historical average of the company's P/E Ratio. If the calculated P/E Ratio is higher than the industry and historical averages, it could mean that the stock is overvalued. On the other hand, if the calculated P/E Ratio is lower than the industry and historical averages, it could mean that the stock is undervalued. We must understand here that this rationale does not always hold good. At times, the markets are in the bull phase and stocks are generally overvalued. On the other hand, bear markets will always drag down the valuations. Hence, the P/E ratio analysis must always be seen in the context of the current market situation. In the chart below, you can see Nifty's P/E chart from 2012.

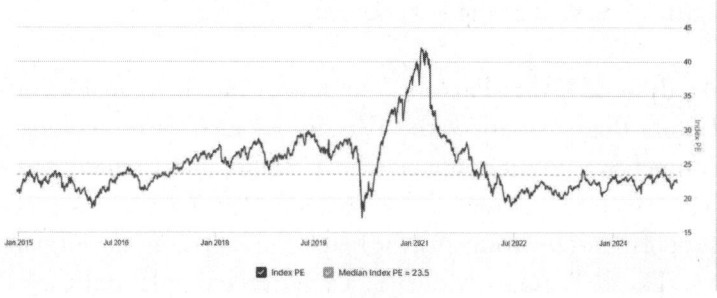

Index PE

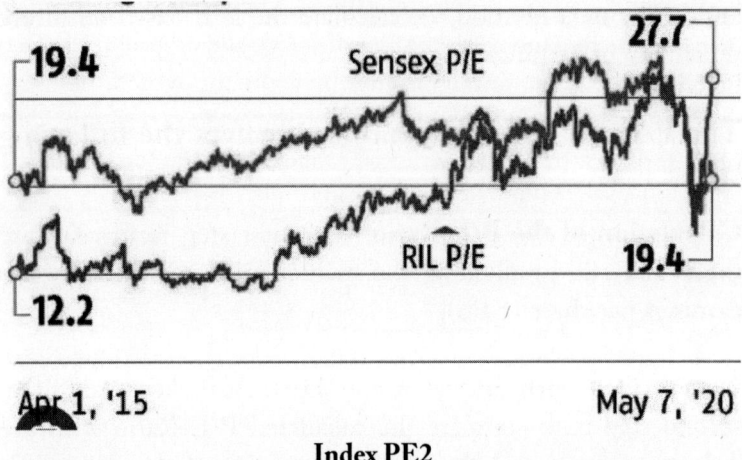

Index PE2

Analysis of the Company's Earnings Status: The third step is to analyse the company's earnings and the earnings growth rate. A high and sustainable earnings growth rate may justify a higher P/E Ratio, while a low or declining earnings growth rate may result in a lower P/E Ratio. In general in the markets, we see that the stocks or sectors which have possibilities of better growth will always be expensive. For example, mid-cap companies which have better growth potential will command higher valuations and will have a higher P/E. One more factor in P/E analysis is the market condition which can be depicted in the chart below. We can see that during COVID-19, the earnings as well as the P/E tanked.

Analysis of Other Factors: The fourth step is to analyse other factors that may affect the P/E Ratio, such as the company's competitive position, management quality and industry trends. These factors are largely market related; the more these factors are supportive of the company, the better the valuations it commands.

The P/E Ratio Model is a relatively simple and easy-to-use equity valuation model in the Indian stock market. It is often used as a quick and rough estimate of the value of a stock.

However, it also has some limitations, including the potential for inaccuracies due to differences in accounting practices and the trust on EPS maintenance by the company, which may not be sustainable. Additionally, the P/E Ratio does not consider the company's future growth potential or risk factors, both of which are very difficult to anticipate.

The formula for the Price to Earnings (P/E) Ratio Model can be written as follows:

P/E Ratio = Market Price per Share / Earnings per Share (EPS)

Where:

P/E Ratio: Price to Earnings Ratio

Market Price per Share: The current market price of a single share of the company's stock

EPS: Earnings per Share, which is calculated by dividing the company's net income with the number of outstanding shares

Price to Book (P/B) Ratio Model: The P/B Ratio Model is another commonly used equity valuation model. It basically estimates the intrinsic value of a stock by comparing its market price to its book value per share. Roughly, the book value per share is the company's total assets minus its liabilities, divided by the number of outstanding shares. Technically speaking, the book value is the accounting technique of calculating the value of a share.

The P/B Ratio is calculated as the market price per share divided by the book value per share. The method is generally used to analyse banking and NBFC stocks.

The P/B Ratio Model involves the following steps:

Calculation of the P/B Ratio: The first step is to calculate the P/B Ratio by dividing the market price per share by the book value per share.

Comparison with Industry and Historical Averages: The second step is to compare the calculated P/B Ratio with the industry average and the historical average of the company's P/B Ratio. If the calculated P/B Ratio is higher than the industry and historical averages, it could mean that the stock is overvalued. On the other hand, if the calculated P/B Ratio is lower than the industry and historical averages, it could mean that the stock is undervalued. The important thing to note here is that just as in the method of calculating the P/E ratio, we must also see the P/B in connection with the current market environment.

Analysis of the Company's Assets: The third step is to analyse the company's assets and asset quality. A high-quality asset base may justify a higher P/B Ratio, while a low-quality asset base may result in a lower P/B Ratio. For instance, if a large part of the company's assets are cash and equivalents, then it may command a higher P/B ratio. On the other hand, if the company has invested most of the amount in risky assets, it will command a lower P/B ratio.

The formula for the Price to Book (P/B) Ratio Model can be written as follows:

P/B Ratio = Market Price per Share / Book Value per Share
Where:
P/B Ratio: Price to Book Ratio
Market Price per Share: The current market price of a single share of the company's stock
Book Value per Share: The Company's total assets minus its liabilities, divided by the number of outstanding shares.

The P/B Ratio Model is a simple and easy-to-use equity valuation model in the Indian stock market. It is often used as a quick and rough estimate of the value of a stock. However, it also has some limitations, as we do not know about the future status of the company's assets. We do not know if the company will be able to realize full value from its assets in the coming days.

Chapter 5

Market Risks and Portfolio Management

Types of Market Risks and Their Impact on Investment Portfolios

Investment is not only about earnings and multiplying your wealth; it is an activity which is fraught with risk too. The path of making money wends its way through various risks which are largely caused by the uncertainty prevalent in the investing environment. This uncertainty decides the quantum of profit or loss on your investments. As Hungarian–American investor George Soros said:

'Risk is when there are multiple possible future states and the probabilities of those different future states occurring are known.'

I personally say that risk is when you know the risk. If you know the risk, you can manage it.

In this section, we will try to understand various kinds of risks associated with investing.

Systemic Risk: This is the risk of a widespread market collapse due to events like economic recession, financial crises, geopolitical tensions, etc. These risks are non-diversifiable and cannot be avoided at all or they are inherent to economics. COVID-19 was a systemic risk associated with equities and other kinds of investment.

Interest Rate Risk: Changes in interest rates impact bond prices inversely. Rising rates can decrease bond values, affecting fixed-income portfolios; on the other hand, rising interest rates are not favourable to equity markets. Any business needs capital with the least cost so that it can generate better ROI. In case of rising interest rates, the ROI of the business would suffer and that will translate into an impact on profits. In recent times, global interest rates are at a multi-year high and that is impacting global equity. Before every Fed meet, the equity markets have reacted and we could see a meltdown in equities after the increase of every basis point in interest rates.

As we can see in the chart below, the day the Fed started raising rates, we could see a meltdown in the US equity markets.

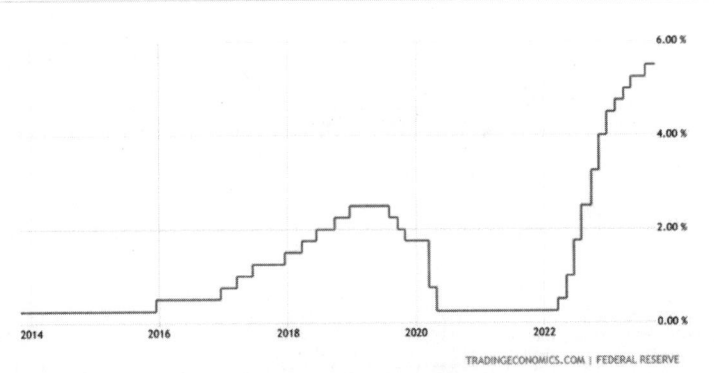

Interest Rate Risk

At the same time, rates in Indian markets are also raised by RBI as the fear of inflation was looming. Since then, the markets are still sceptical about the near-term future of equities. In the chart below, we can see the rate chart of Repo by RBI. It is quite notable that during COVID-19, the rates were taken to 4 per cent which was a multi-year low and now when there is a fear of inflation, the rates are higher than they were in the pre-COVID era. These rates are quite negative for sectors like auto, banking and real estate. These sectors will always be prone to risks associated with interest rates.

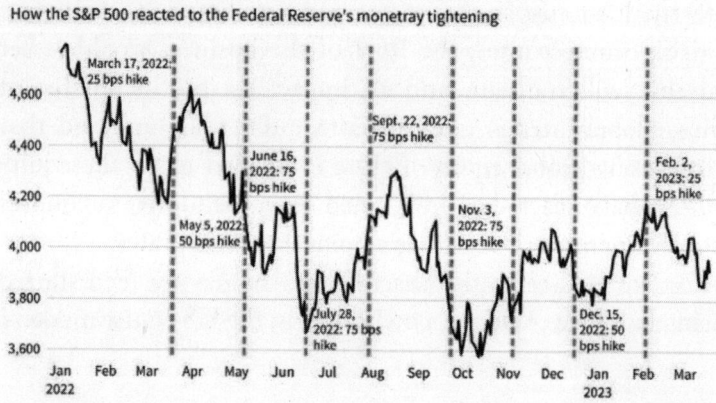

Rate Hikes

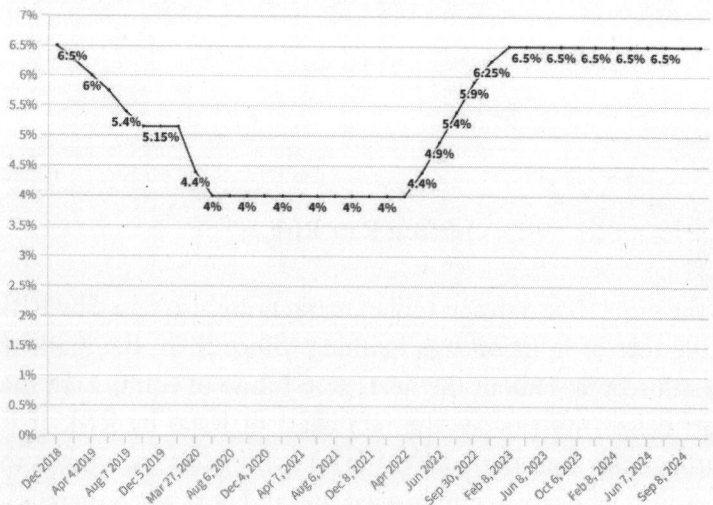

RBI Rate Hike

Currency Risk: From the dollar to the yen, we have seen global currencies getting volatile so many times; their impact on stocks has been quite dangerous for equity. Recently we have seen that the dollar index has been quite volatile and the impact on global equities has been quite negative. This particular risk has been emerging due to the globalization of the equity markets. Most of the world equity markets are invested with foreign capital and any movement in global currency markets will impact the equities too. We can also see the stocks of oil companies like BPCL, IOCL, HPCL and others, as we import most of our crude oil and we must pay in dollars. Any further upward movement in dollar price will make life difficult for crude importers.

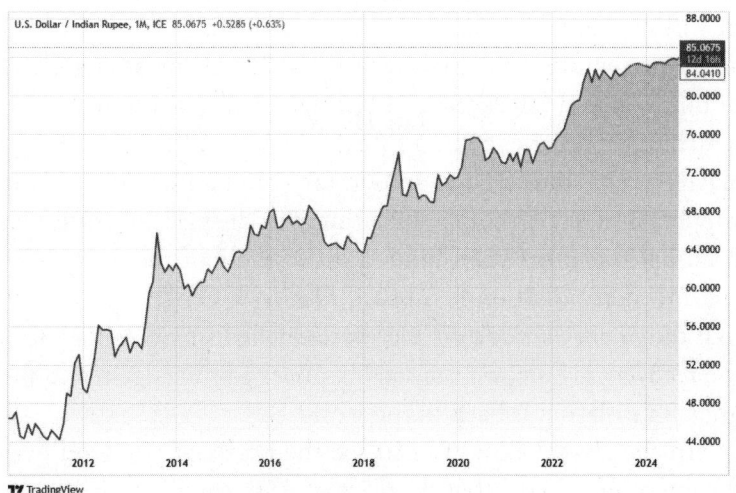

Currency Risk 1

The above charts depict the conversion of the dollar to the rupee and the chart on the right-hand side tells us about the value of the dollar index which is technically the price of the dollar for a basket of currency. We can see that in recent times, the dollar index has shot up and that has posed quite a risk for global equities.

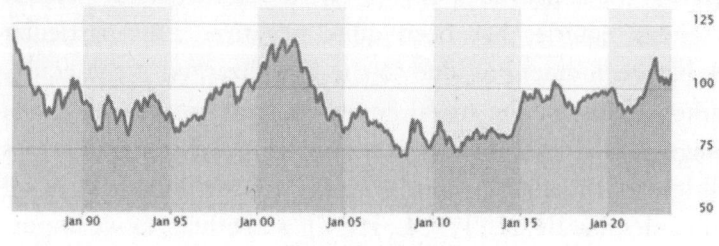

Currency Risk 2

Commodity Risk: Prices of commodities like oil, gold or agricultural products can be volatile, affecting investments in various sectors. Although commodity is a risk, it does not affect the equities directly; instead it takes shape as the ghost of inflation and forces the Central Banks to raise interest rates, which in turn proves to be a threat to equities. Investors should always track some of the important commodities like crude, copper, steel, etc. A single dollar jump in the price of crude will push up global inflation quite a bit as most of the economies are now dependent on fossil fuel. During COVID-19, we saw that the prices of crude oil had even touched single digits but as the recovery is here, we can see the prices gaining again and the ghost of inflation is back in the world.

In the chart below, we can see the prices of crude oil over the years. We can see that the price of crude touched an all-time high in 2008. That was when global markets were facing the double pressure of equity meltdown and higher inflation.

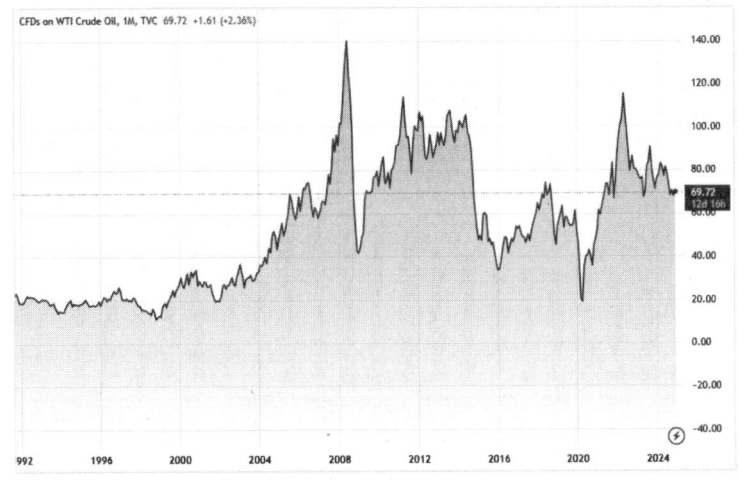

CFDs on WTI Crude Oil, 1M, TVC 69.72 +1.61 (+2.36%)

Commodity Risk

Liquidity Risk: The world of equity runs on the fuel of liquidity. Sometimes the liquidity is more significant than the fundamentals of the market. We have often seen that during times of better liquidity, the markets keep galloping on, irrespective of earnings. On the other hand, a tighter liquidity scenario, like the current times, sees the market taking a nosedive.

For example, we saw during COVID-19 when the US was seemingly printing dollars, the markets were flushed with funds and global equities were scaling new heights. On the other hand, there is the scenario of late 2022 to 2023 when all the central banks were hawkish on liquidity. Due to the risk of inflation, equities were quite reluctant, even though corporate earnings were at an all-time high.

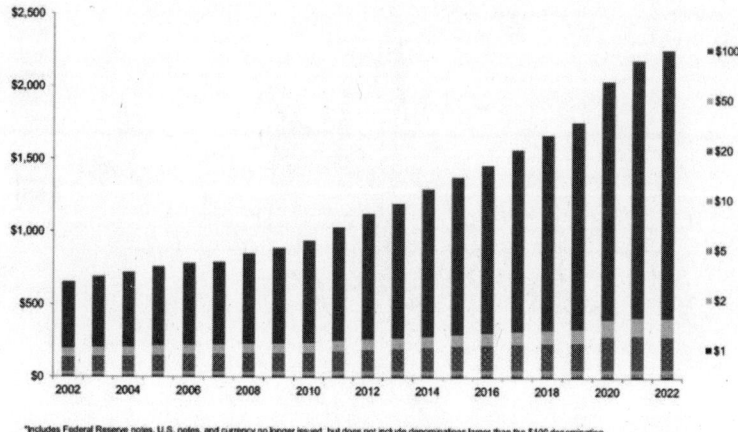

*Includes Federal Reserve notes, U.S. notes, and currency no longer issued, but does not include denominations larger than the $100 denomination.

Liquidity Risk

In the above chart, the currency in circulation in the US went up by around 40 per cent from 2019–22. We all know that it was a great time for global equities. Another important part of liquidity is the prevailing interest rates. The lower the interest rates, the better is the liquidity in the markets; higher interest rates provide better liquidity to equity. We have seen the mechanism and details of interest rates in the above section.

Political and Regulatory Risk: In the current scenario of global diplomacy, the world political risk to equity is an important factor. In recent times, we have seen that the day the Ukraine–Russia war erupted, the equity markets reacted negatively; the commodity market especially was on the boil. On the other hand, regulatory risk is also an important factor to be considered. Certain regulatory changes can put some companies out of the business. One recent example of this is GST implementation on casinos and online gaming. As per the ruling, the gaming and casino companies had to pay 18 per cent GST on the gross amount. Companies like Nazara and Delta reacted negatively to the news.

Credit Risk: We have heard the names of Fannie Mae and Freddie Mac, home mortgage companies. During the 2008 crisis, both companies went bankrupt due to credit default by a number of home owners in the US market. This created a spiral of default around the world and led to one of the worst financial crises historically. In the chart below, we can see that the biggest jolt came from sub-prime lending in 2008. Traders or investors should always keep an eye on the amount of credit in different segments of the economy, especially credit involved in unsecured areas like credit cards, etc. Below in the chart on the right-hand side, we can see the US credit card debt over a period of time

Mortgage Delinquency

Informational Risk: This type of risk has never been on the list historically, but nowadays we have seen the rise of information about equities due to the rise of social media, with thousands of influencers coming to the fore. Investors and traders should always be aware about the nature of the information and knowledge supplied to them. The wrong information, translated into investment, can pose a huge risk, especially to small investors.

The impact of these risks on an investment portfolio varies based on factors like the investor's risk tolerance, investment goals and asset allocation. Diversification, proper risk management and a long-term investment perspective can help mitigate the effects of these risks. A common investor must also understand that the impact of risk will vary as per the size of the investors. The risks which are problematic to small investors can be quite normal for a large investor as they have their own requirements and type of investments. One recent example of this is the fallout from COVID-19, when the long-term institutional investors kept their investments but the retail investors could not handle the situation well as prices crashed instantly.

Portfolio Construction and Management Strategies

This is probably the first stage of wealth creation; if the portfolio is well constituted and thought out, then half the job is done. The advantage of having a well-constructed portfolio is that you don't have to churn it regularly; the portfolio sails through good and bad times. In this section, we will try to understand the nuances of a good portfolio and understand the process of creating one. The following are important aspects of a good portfolio:

Diversification: As the old saying 'Don't put all your eggs in one basket' advises, as an investor or trader, it is essential to spread investments across different asset classes (stocks, bonds, real estate, etc.) to reduce risk. So if one asset class does not perform well, the other one can. This theory is largely based on the premise that in an economy, all sectors, and in a sector, all companies, do not perform well together. We can have sectoral diversification as well as company-wise diversification in a sector. For example, at a particular time you can have banks, petrochem, speciality chemicals, etc. in your portfolio. To take it further, if you want to add weightage to a particular sector, say, banks, you may have SBI as PSU, HDFC as a private bank and even RBL as a mid-cap bank.

Asset Allocation: Another important part of portfolio diversification is having various asset classes in your portfolio. One important thing to take care of while choosing commodities is that we should go for those which are less volatile. Gold and silver are comparatively less volatile than copper, etc. It is important to determine the mix of different asset classes in the portfolio, based on goals, risk tolerance and the investment horizon. This can help manage risks while aiming for the desired returns. While deciding about the asset allocation, we need to be very particular about our own risk profile. What suits a person aged twenty-five might not suit a person aged forty. At the same time, your location, lifestyle, life goals, etc. are also very important when deciding about asset allocation.

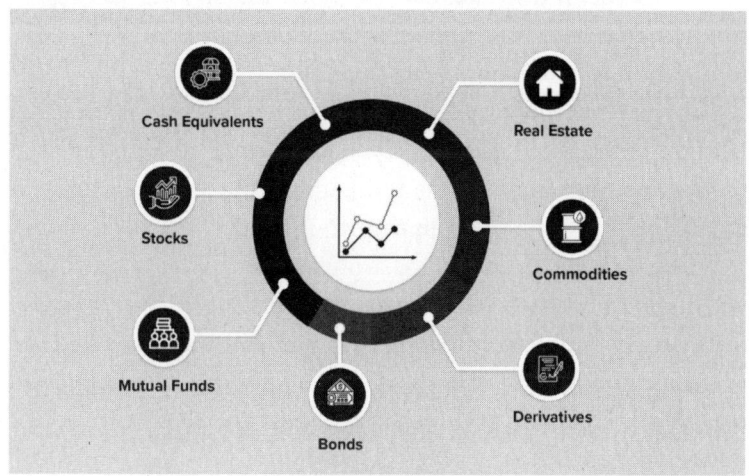

Asset Allocation

Risk Tolerance: There is no standard method or machine to analyse the risk tolerance capacity of a particular investor or trader. It depends on a lot of factors, most importantly on personal preference. As per the age factor, we might not advise a person over sixty to trade in futures and options but if the person is affluent, he can trade or invest in any instrument of his choice.

The risk tolerance also depends on the knowledge of the investors. For example, when COVID-19 struck the world, real estate prices around the country started falling as a lot of people started selling their assets in panic. At the same time, those who understood real estate markets well kept on buying real estate and made a lot of money when life became normal again. One important advice to all investors is that they should not take aggressive calls and should not go beyond their risk-taking capabilities while investing.

Timeline of investing: We invest because we want to earn money for a particular future requirement. These goals will differ for every individual investor. Focusing on long-term goals can help ride out short-term market fluctuations and reduce the temptation to make impulsive decisions.

If you need money for the wedding of your son or daughter who is five years old right now, you can always go for equities as the requirement is quite long term and, in the long run, equity is a good wealth generator. On the other hand, if you need money to make a down payment for a house which you want to buy within the next two to three years, you should always go for debt products and fixed deposits as you will want to avoid the volatility of equity. In the short run, equity can even take a hit on the principal and you might not meet the requirement of a down payment.

For the same purpose, if we talk about the investment strategies of large players, it's always for the long run. A mutual fund would never like to go for low risk–low return companies as a large part of their investments is mandated for the long run, which increases the risk appetite for a common investor.

Rebalancing: Investing is a journey and while travelling, you end up quite far from where you started. What this means is that you don't stay with the same companies in your portfolio forever. Periodically adjusting the portfolio back to the original asset allocation helps maintain the desired risk levels. Selling assets that have performed well and buying those that have underperformed can keep the portfolio in line with your goals. A hundred years ago, gold was considered as the best investment tool as there were very few options. But now when we have many asset classes, the strategy has changed, and active investors are chasing equity more than ever.

Another important part of rebalancing involves changing the allocation to the asset mix in the portfolio. You may have heard various portfolio managers saying that they are either bearish or bullish on a particular asset class; that view changes as the economic environment changes.

Active Versus Passive Management: This is a very important part of portfolio management. We usually see passive investors investing either in index funds or blue-chip companies. Passive investors do not want to spend time researching investing avenues. They would like to settle for an average rate of return. On the other hand, active management involves trying to outperform the market through research and frequent trading. Passive management involves tracking a market index. Both approaches have their pros and cons. An active portfolio management is based on regular research and timely rebalancing of the portfolio. Index funds and exchange-traded funds (ETFs) are the best examples of passive portfolio management. As we can see in the picture below, growth in ETFs and index funds has been phenomenal over the years. One important reason for this is the growth in overall Assets Under Management of the industry. Another important factor is the market volatility. If you perceive that markets are going to be volatile, as a prudent investor, a passive portfolio is a good strategy.

However, retail participation is on rise
(Retail investors' folio growth (in numbers) in overall ETFs and index funds)

ETFs — 468%

Index Funds — 362%

Source: AMFI.

Retailers

Tax Efficiency: Tax is the last factor in accounting entries but it is the most important factor while making an investment. Considering tax implications when making investment decisions can help minimize tax liabilities. Strategies include tax-efficient fund selection and tax-loss harvesting. Sometimes tax differences can change the overall return mathematics. For example, in the case of mutual funds investment, the dividend received from equity funds is taxable at the rate of the tax bracket of the investors, but when they redeem the units, the investors are taxed at the rate of 20 per cent as the gain is considered as short-term capital gain on the equity instrument. In this case, if your overall tax liability is less than 20 per cent, you should opt for the dividend option in equity mutual funds. Else, you should go for growth funds and redeem the amount whenever you need it.

There are many instances where tax becomes the final deciding factor for investing decisions. For example, in the earlier regime, long-term capital gain taxation on Fixed Maturity Plan (FMP) and Fixed Deposits (FD) was a much discussed point. The FDs were taxed as per the investor's tax bracket whereas the returns from the FMPs were taxed as debt instruments. This led to people from higher tax brackets and companies investing only in FMPs. ULIPs, being 100 per cent tax exempted, became an attractive option to invest in.

Liquidity Management: This should be the most important part of the investment strategy. Sometimes we are so obsessed with the investment that we forget about our short-term needs. If you have been trading in the markets for ten to fifteen years and if the markets crashed more than 30 per cent, you would not mind borrowing in order to invest because as per your experience, finally the markets will rebound and give fantastic returns.

The danger in investing, lest the investor forget, is that in the case of volatile investments, we might not withdraw the funds when we need them. It generally happens in the case of property too as the ticket size is very high. While investing, we should always ensure that we don't invest all the funds we have at our disposal. Having some liquid cash is always a good idea. You must always ensure that you have enough liquid assets to cover short-term needs. This helps prevent the need to sell investments at unfavourable times.

Scenario Analysis and Stress Testing: This tool becomes very useful when the investing markets become volatile. Most of the time we invest on an understanding that things will go well, but no one can control future outcomes. We should always evaluate how the portfolio might perform under different market conditions. This helps us assess risks and potential outcomes. Uninformed investors might find it hard to evaluate this, but nowadays there are many statistical tools which allow you to understand various outcomes based on certain back testing and other tools.

Seasoned investors should always be prepared for the 'worst case scenario' which is the limit of the non-performance of the portfolio. This allows them to manage the timeline of the investment and manage the liquidity scenario.

Investment in Knowledge: Learning before doing is quite important and we need to understand the market well before making an investment. Continually educating yourself about financial markets, investment strategies and economic trends can empower you to make informed decisions. You, as an investor, will be more aware about your decisions and will not rely completely on a third party. The best part about this is that nowadays there are thousands of channels, social media handles and tools that are available in the market to supply good information on a regular basis.

Knowledge helps in settling exuberance. After the 2020 crash and the subsequent rebound, everyone wants to make money from the stock markets. The investors who have entered the market after the 2020 crash have not seen the crash of 2008, which was much fiercer. Some of them believe that making money from the stock markets is the easiest thing in the world. Every investor should understand this issue well and should not get influenced by market voices. No matter which phase you enter the markets, you should study it well. Always make an informed decision. As per a recent SEBI report, nine out of ten F&O traders lose money. I believe that this is so because they don't study the market well but start trading by getting influenced by the market voices.

Although we have tried to cover maximum aspects of investment strategies, one must remember that there can be no one-size-fits-all approach. Portfolios should be tailored to individual circumstances, financial goals and risk tolerance. Regular adjustments and a disciplined approach are key to successful portfolio management. We should know what we want from our portfolio and on that basis, the portfolio must be created.

Chapter 6

Common Mistakes by Stock Traders and Investors

To start with, let us understand two basic fundamental pointers to be kept in mind before buying any stock. These are the bare minimum requirements.

EPS Growth Rate: EPS is the single most important criteria while selecting a winning stock. We should look for an EPS growth rate of over 18 per cent quarter on quarter and year on year.

A company can generate earnings in various ways, some not so honourable. I prefer high-quality earnings. In other words, where do the earnings come from? Did the company post better results because of stronger sales? If sales were strong, was it only because of a single product or one major customer? In that case, the growth is vulnerable. Or are the surprisingly strong results due to an industry-wide phenomenon or an influx of orders from numerous buyers? Maybe the company is slashing costs and cutting back. Earnings improvement from cost-cutting, plant closures and other so-called productivity enhancements walks on short legs. Such improvements can show up from time to time, but sustainable earnings growth requires revenue growth. So along with the EPS growth rate, we need to check the quality of the earnings as well to ensure that it is sustainable over time.

Beware of management communications as they have learnt how to manage expectations. One gimmick is to warn the public of a potential earnings problem, which will cause analysts to lower their earnings estimates. Then the company reports earnings that are better than the lowered estimate. This will result in an earnings surprise; however, it will be a surprise in the context of a lower consensus comparison. So beware of what is happening around and don't take anything at face value.

Also, beware—the company may be increasing its profits by reducing the expenses. A company can increase profits by cutting jobs, closing plants or shedding its losing operations. However, these measures have a limited lifespan. Eventually, a company will have to do something else to grow its business and increase its top line. Therefore, check the story behind the earnings growth.

The ideal situation is when a company has higher sales volume with new or current products in new and existing markets as well as higher prices and reduced costs. That's a winning combination of a winner stock.

For example, let me show you the ten biggest wealth creators from 2018 to 2023. Just check the PAT CAGR and Return on Equity (ROE) of the majority of these stocks. ROE is the measure of a company's net income divided by its shareholders' equity. ROE is a gauge of a corporation's profitability and how efficiently it generates those profits. Below is the list of the top ten most consistently performing stocks of the last five years:

Rank	Company	No. of years of outperformance	2018-23 Price CAGR (%)	2018-23 PAT CAGR (%)	RoE (%) 2023	RoE (%) 2018
1	Capri Global	5	50	26	6	5
2	Varun Beverages	5	50	50	31	12
3	Grindwell Norton	5	30	19	19	15
4	ICICI Bank	5	26	35	16	7
5	Adani Enterprises	4	78	34	7	4
6	Tube Investments	4	63	53	33	12
7	Linde India	4	56	91	17	1
8	Adani Power	4	52	L to P	36	N.M.
9	J B Chem	4	45	31	16	7
10	SRF	4	44	36	21	13

Sales Growth Rate: The EPS growth rate is sustainable if it is combined with the sales growth rate. We look for 18 per cent CAGR sales growth rate, quarter on quarter and year on year too.

For beginners, these two can be the initial filters to look out for while selecting any stock.

Stock trading is not an easy task. We all want to earn a lot of money from it but it takes a disciplined approach to do so. It is easier said than done as historically we have seen that even the best investors cannot avoid making mistakes while trading. In this section, we will talk about the most common mistakes which are part of the trading approach of a large number of traders and investors.

1. **Trying to catch the falling knife**: This is probably the most common mistake. Most traders and investors are obsessed with the so-called all-time high price of a particular stock. This is why when a particular stock falls, some investors keep buying it without analysing the reasons for the fall. This generally works as a trap for investors; they keep buying at lower prices and the stock keeps falling. Investors must strictly avoid this approach and always analyse the reason why the stock is falling. Always remember, only a loser buys a losing stock. If you find yourself in a hole, stop digging. Always set yourself a rule of maximum loss of 8 per cent in one stock position. Also, when you average down, you forget the principle of portfolio sizing and end up having 25–30 per cent++ in a single portfolio because of which now your portfolio returns will be completely dependent on the performance of a single stock.

Also, if your stock falls 20 per cent, it has to rise 25 per cent to reach its cost. If the stock falls 25 per cent, it has to rise 33 per cent to reach its cost. If a stock falls 50 per cent, you need 100 per cent returns to reach your cost. Hence, never try to catch a falling knife.

2. **Not cutting your losses:** As a part of the portfolio, an investor must always keep track of where he is losing and earning. Getting back to your paid price is sometimes just a game of hope; this is why most investors don't want to cut their losses, even if they are very small. They need to understand that the capital which is stuck in the loss-making trade can be utilized for some other trade to earn better returns. Many people think that presently they just have a loss in the books and that as soon as they book it, it will be their booked loss. Our mind treats booked loss versus loss in books differently, but in reality, we need to understand that both are mathematically the same and hence should be treated in the same way.

3. **Afraid of buying at a higher price:** If you study the charts well, you will understand that there is something called a breakout. Sometimes, a stock performs well and goes up with huge volumes because it is about to give a breakout which will take it even higher. Investors don't understand this properly and think that the stock is going to fall soon. But actually the opposite happens. As the stock has given a breakout, it will continue to rise and the investor will lose an opportunity. The biggest psychological reason for the same is recency bias. We feel that a stock which was available at Rs 300 is now available at Rs 330, so there is no use buying it and we keep waiting for the price to come back to Rs 300.

Usually if it's a good breakout, it will never reach that level. And when it does, then probably the trend has reversed already and the juice in the fruit is drained.

4. **Selecting stock due to lower valuations:** In a universe of more than 4000 stocks listed in India, you will find at least 200 stocks which are trading at less than 10 Price to Earnings Ratio (PE) which makes them very attractive to invest in theoretically. Before putting any money in those stocks, we need to understand why these stocks are trading at lower valuations. The reason is simple: it is because of the company's performance. The company does not have the potential to perform well in future. The market is not ready to give a better valuation to them. Ask yourself: Is a particular stock available at a cheap PE or is it a cheap stock in itself? If you pay too much heed to the PE of a stock, you can never be a growth investor or trader. Although it may come as a surprise to you, historical analyses of superperformance stocks suggest that by themselves, P/E ratios rank among the most useless statistics. The standard P/E ratio reflects historical results and does not take into account the most important element for stock price appreciation: the future. Sure, it's possible to use earnings estimates to calculate a forward-looking P/E ratio, but if you do, you're relying on estimates that are opinions that often turn out to be wrong. If a company reports disappointing earnings that fail to meet or beat the estimates, analysts will revise their earnings projections downward. As a result, the forward-looking denominator—the E in P/E—will shrink and, assuming the P remains constant, the ratio will rise. This is why it is important to concentrate on companies

that are reporting strong earnings, which then trigger upward revisions in earnings estimates. Strong earnings growth will make a stock a better value.

5. **Buying a low PE stock just because it has low PE is like falling into a trap:** Buying a cheap stock is like a trap hand in poker; it's hard to get away from it. When you buy a stock solely because it's cheap, it's difficult to sell if it moves against you because then it's even cheaper, which is the reason you bought it in the first place. The cheaper it gets, the more attractive it becomes based on the 'it's cheap' rationale. This is the type of thinking that gets investors in big trouble. Most investors look for bargains, instead of looking for leaders, and more often than not, they get what they pay for.

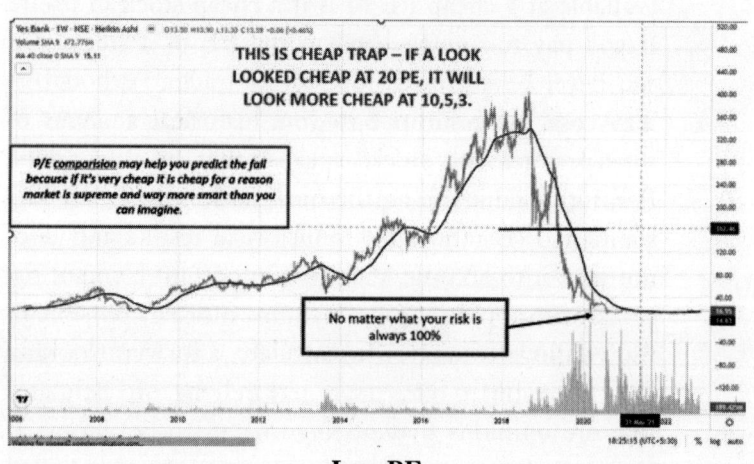

Low PE

Everybody knows the old adage, 'Buy low and sell high'. It makes sense—like going to a store to find something on sale. However, buying low and selling high has little to do with the current stock price. How high or low the price is relative to where it was previously is not the determining factor in whether a stock will go higher still. A stock trading at Rs 800 can go to Rs 3000, just as a stock trading at Rs 50 can go to Rs 5 or even to zero.

Low PE1

6. **Tips can be rumour-based:** Most traders come to market to make fast money and that takes them to the route of buying on tips. They are generally rumour-based and sometime investors lose a large amount of money on them. We have seen retail investors falling prey to this. There are only a few incidents where we find these tips really working. Else, most of the time they fail and cause investors to lose money. The actual full form of TIPS is, according to me, **T**o fool **I**nnocent **P**eople in **S**tocks.

7. **Bad selling approach:** Some investors have a very good buying strategy and style but they get defeated by a bad selling approach to the stocks. This generally happens on both sides, sometimes when the stock keeps falling and, on the other hand, when it keeps rising. Booking losses and profits both are essential elements of the markets and must be done on time. To

sell, we must have both a stop loss and a target for profit. Whatever comes first must be executed. If you don't know how and when to exit, you will always be dissatisfied with the stock market returns. Would you enter a tunnel without knowing how to get out? Would you sit in a plane if you have no surety of landing? Would you drive a car which has no brake? Then why would you enter a stock where you have no idea how and when you will exit? Even if your stop-loss hits and you exit, it is absolutely okay. Hitting a stop-loss is no crime; it is like an insurance which will ensure that you stay in the game called stock market in the long term. And, as it happens in cricket where, if you stay on the crease, runs automatically start coming, in the same way, if you stay in the stock market for the long term, automatically the market will give you the opportunity to make money. The key is to stay in the game for the long term. The data says that 95 per cent of traders lose money. My question is, how many of them survived in the market for more than five years? Staying in the market for more than five years should be your goal.

8. **Not able to identify the new kids on the block:** This is called proximity bias. Most investors try to trade and invest in some familiar names only. For example, Indian traders try to trade in Nifty stocks but we need to understand that there is a lot of value beyond this. Probable multibaggers come from a broader universe of markets. This is a perfect scenario of familiarity bias. For example, you will always see that an old trader coming back to the market after a gap will always search for old names and will be more comfortable in investing or trading in them. But in reality, the maximum juice is

always available in new fruits (stocks) which have come into the market in the last two years. Consider it like a forest, where the fire destroyed everything (the stock market crash happened) and now again, new trees will grow. Some of the old trees might be able to sustain themselves but at the same time, a lot of newer trees are strengthening their base.

9. **Quick Money:** Futures and options are very quick on both sides. They make quick money as well as cause quick bankruptcies. We need to understand that F&O trading is a highly specialized job and must be taken up when you are extremely confident about your trade set-up. In India, we generally see that traders mostly trade on the basis of intuition, which is very detrimental while dealing in F&O. I don't say that F&O is a 'no go' but you must touch them only when you are a highly trained trader. Following quick-rich theories will make you poor quickly. Even as a beginner, if you want to do futures and options, then strategies like covered call or vertical credit are to be used.

A covered call gives someone else the right to purchase stock shares that you already own at a specified price (strike price) and at any time on or before a specified date (expiration date). By owning the stock, you're 'covered' (i.e., protected) if the stock rises and the call option expires. Here you own the stock and sell out of the money calls to earn a regular income. For example, if you have Reliance stock at Rs 3000 and the current market price is also Rs 3000 and you want to do a covered call, then you will sell OTM calls at Rs 3200 or Rs 3300, according to your strategy, liquidity and framework. In summary, a covered call is constructed by holding a long position in a stock and then selling (writing) call options on that same asset, representing the same size as the underlying long position. It will limit the investor's potential upside profit but at the same time, it reduces the effective cost of the asset by generating a regular income.

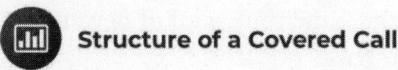

Structure of a Covered Call

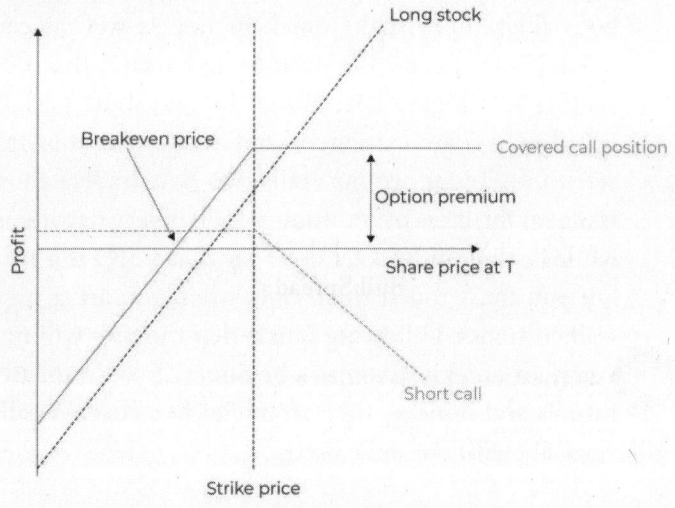

Covered Call

Vertical spread options are a directional trading strategy that involves simultaneously buying and selling the same option type (call or put) with the same expiration date but different strike prices. The goal of using a vertical spread is to limit potential losses while still allowing for potential profits. For example, if you are bullish on Reliance, which is trading at Rs 3000, then you will sell 2900 put and buy 2800 put. Which means that you are selling put OTM and buying put further OTM. In the same way, if you are bearish, then you will sell call at Rs 3100 and buy Reliance call of Rs 3200.

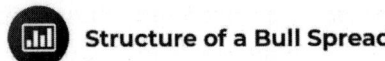 **Structure of a Bull Spread**

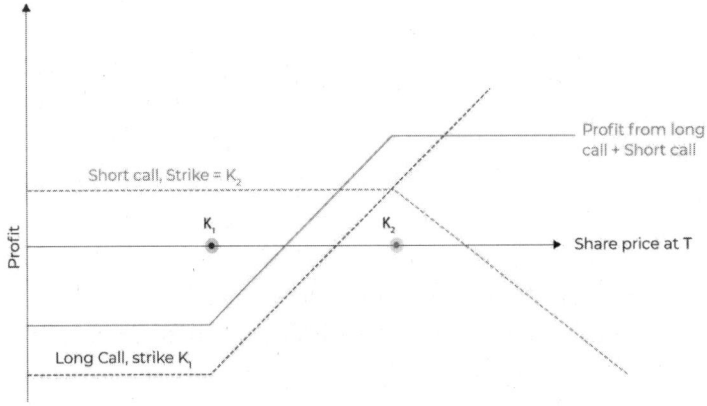

Bull Spread

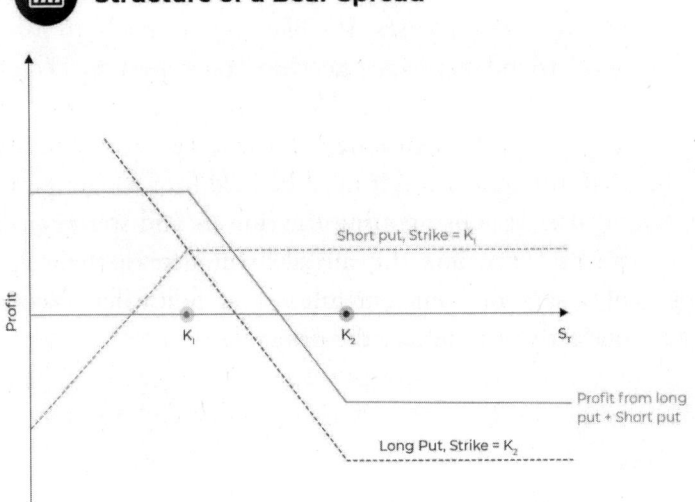

Bear Spread

10. **Emotional attachment:** We need to understand that the stock market is about hardcore money and there is no place to get emotional. Sometimes traders stick to their favourite stock even if does not make good money for them. A lot of traders would like to trade in ITC only because they feel that this a good blue-chip stock and a good tradable thing. Here we need to understand that ITC can be a good investment stock but for trading, it is not a preferred option. In the same way, many are stuck with names like Yes Bank, DHFL, Vodafone, Indus Tower, etc.

11. **Selling performers and holding on to losers:** If an investor has ten stocks in his portfolio and, say, in three stocks, he has doubled his money and in three, he is losing around 30 per cent. This is generally seen as a tendency that the investors will sell the performing stock first and will keep holding the non-performing one under the expectation that it will rise some day and will recover its losses. It's like you are ready to lose a good friend for someone who you expect to become a good friend someday. We must understand that the good stock is performing because it has better potential than the others and it must be held for a longer period of time. It is like cutting the flowers and watering the weeds. Over time, this mistake will increase the weight of losers in your portfolio. The following diagram perfectly summarizes the principle:

The disposition effect

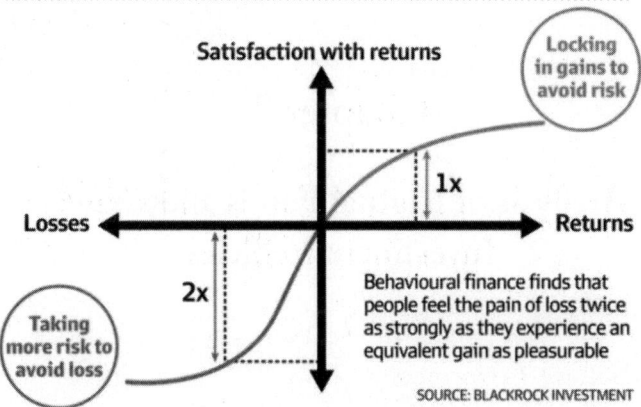

Disposition Effect

Chapter 7

Analysis of Mutual Funds and Other Investment Vehicles

Over the years, mutual funds have been a great wealth creator for all categories of investors. Those who are aggressive in their investing style have funds in the small cap and mid cap category, those who want to get into blue-chip only can opt for large cap funds, passive investors can go for index funds, and an investor who doesn't want to be part of equity at all can opt for debt funds or FPMs. Even gold funds are available. Name any type of investment vehicle, and a mutual fund will be available in the markets.

Technically, mutual funds are investment vehicles that pool money from multiple investors to purchase a diversified portfolio of stocks, bonds or other securities. They offer individual investors a convenient way to access professional management and diversification, even with relatively small amounts of money. You can even start monthly with Rs 500 in mutual funds. It is quite notable that the AUM of the Indian MF Industry has grown from Rs 7.66 trillion as on 31 August 2013 to Rs 46.63 trillion as on 31 August 2023, a more than sixfold increase in a span of ten years. In the chart below, we can see how the mutual funds industry has been growing in India.

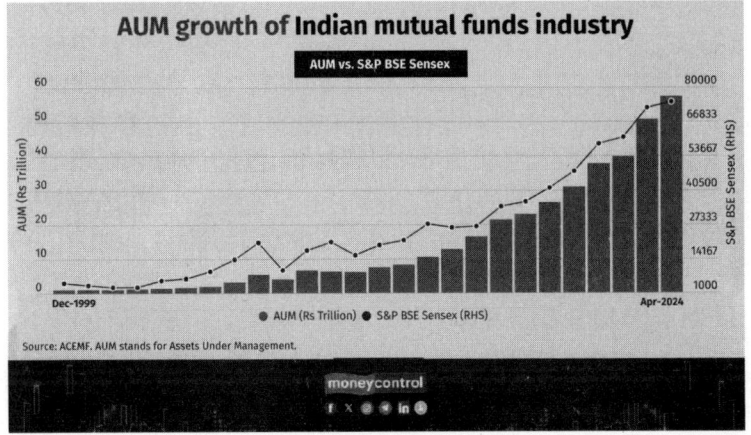

AUM Growth

Types of Mutual Funds

In India and in global markets, different types of mutual funds are available, each catering to different investment objectives and risk profiles. Here are some common types of mutual funds available in India:

Equity Funds: The most talked about and sought after category of mutual funds is equity mutual funds. These funds invest primarily in equity stocks and try to maximize the investors' wealth in the long run. On the basis of the company they invest in, equity funds can be further classified into small cap, mid cap, large cap and flexi cap. Technically, equity mutual funds are available for every class and type of investor. The size of the equity mutual funds industry is around Rs 17 lakh crore, as we can see in the table below. There are a total of 397 schemes available from various fund houses and the number of schemes is ever growing.

Sr No.	Scheme Name	No. of Schemes as on 30 June 2023	Average Net Assets Under Management for the month of June 2023 (INR in crore)
	Growth/Equity Oriented Schemes		
i	Multi Cap Fund	19	76,283.71
ii	Large Cap Fund	31	2,54,471.92
iii	Large & Mid Cap Fund	26	1,44,273.15
iv	Mid Cap Fund	29	2,11,811.37
v	Small Cap Fund	24	1,62,184.19
vi	Dividend Yield Fund	9	15,669.63
vii	Value Fund/ Contra Fund	23	1,01,451.32
viii	Focused Fund	27	1,07,903.80
ix	Sectoral/ Thematic Funds	130	1,91,586.55
x	ELSS	43	1,67,341.38
xi	Flexi Cap Fund	36	2,66,987.02
Total		397	16,99,964.04

Debt Funds: Debt mutual funds invest in fixed-income securities like government bonds, corporate bonds and money market instruments. They aim to provide regular income with relatively lower risk, compared to equity funds. In markets like India, debts funds are largely used as a treasury tool and not as an investment opportunity. Corporates park their funds in such tools to maintain their cash flows and generate some returns on it. The following table tells you about the volume of investments in various debt funds. Here, we can see that the highest amount has gone to liquid funds because the amount is largely of treasury operations.

Sr No.	Scheme Name	No. of Schemes as on 30 June 2023	Average Net Assets Under Management for the month of June 2023 (INR in crore)
i	Overnight Fund	32	1,04,201.60
ii	Liquid Fund	36	4,97,239.17
iii	Ultra Short Duration Fund	25	99,418.43
iv	Low Duration Fund	21	96,792.69
v	Money Market Fund	22	1,38,006.29
vi	Short Duration Fund	25	99,209.53
vii	Medium Duration Fund	15	27,483.14
viii	Medium to Long Duration Fund	12	9,900.76
ix	Long Duration Fund	7	9,254.31
x	Dynamic Bond Fund	22	30,166.17
xi	Corporate Bond Fund	21	1,35,233.24
xii	Credit Risk Fund	15	24,479.58
xiii	Banking and PSU Fund	23	82,064.98
xiv	Gilt Fund	22	22,504.66
xv	Gilt Fund with ten-year constant duration	5	4,233.98
xvi	Floater Fund	13	56,859.02
	Total	**316**	**14,37,047.55**

Hybrid Funds: Also known as balanced funds, these funds invest in a mix of both equities and debt instruments. They aim to provide a balance between capital appreciation and income generation. There is always a class of investors who want to have a balance of debt and equity in their portfolio. The investors want to have a balance in risk and return. These kinds of funds are largely chosen by conservative investors who want to take risks with equities but with a contained risk.

Money Market Funds: These funds invest in very short-term debt instruments like treasury bills and commercial paper. They are considered low risk and suitable for short-term parking of funds. These funds are also highly preferred by the treasury operations as they are needed to park additional funds available.

Index Funds: Index funds are probably the most used passive type of funds. These funds replicate a specific stock market index (like Nifty Fifty or Sensex) by investing in the same proportion of stocks as the index. They aim to generate the same return as per the index's performance. Index funds will largely replicate the major indices as Nifty, Sensex, Nifty Mid cap and Nifty Small Cap. In India, we have certain sectoral indices like Nifty Pharma, Nifty Metal, etc. These funds are preferred as a great SIP tool to get the advantage of continuous market fluctuations. One of the best advantages of index funds is that these are passive funds and have a very low cost of management. At times, index funds are unable to replicate the investment in various stocks as per their weight in the indices. That difference is called tracking error which is allowed at a certain percentage only.

Exchange-Traded Funds (ETFs): Similar to index funds, ETFs trade on stock exchanges like individual stocks. They offer diversification and can track various indices or sectors.

Sectoral and Thematic Funds: These funds invest in specific sectors (like banking, technology) or themes (like infrastructure, consumption trends). These funds are used by those investors who like to invest in a particular sector or theme. Usually, sectoral funds are not favoured by investors as historically, not many sectoral funds have been able to generate great returns. Even for fund managers, it is quite difficult to gauge the movement of sectors. Sometimes a particular sector does not generate returns for a very long term and then someday starts doing wonders. A recent example of this is the power sector which did not generate returns for a long period and then suddenly in 2023, the prices of a number of power stocks touched the roof.

Tax-Saving Funds (ELSS): Equity Linked Savings Schemes (ELSS) offer tax benefits under Section 80C of the Income Tax Act. They have a lock-in period of three years and invest primarily in equities. Being locked funds and close-ended in nature, they give the fund manager autonomy to invest freely as they know about the minimum timeline of withdrawal. Currently, the average assets under management of ELSS funds are around Rs 1.7 lakh crore.

Gilt Funds: These funds invest in government securities (gilts). They are considered low risk as they are backed by the government, but returns might be relatively lower as the funds are in the safest hands and that marks the favourable risk–return for the investor.

Gold Funds/Gold ETFs: These funds invest in gold, providing an indirect way to invest in the precious metal without owning physical gold. These funds are preferred nowadays as it makes it easy for the investor to buy gold, even for Rs 500, which would not have been possible if you were to go out to buy physical gold. This is an option which has helped gold investors.

International Funds: These funds invest in international markets, allowing Indian investors to access global equities or bonds. In general, there are not many funds which invest their 100 per cent AUM in international equities but as per regulations, they are allowed to invest a certain percentage in international equities. Since this is now allowed by SEBI, local investors can also benefit from the quality of international stocks.

Winning Strategy on MF: Why Mutual Funds Are the Best Investment Tools

Diversification: The best part of investing in mutual funds is that it proves the truth of that old saying, 'Don't put all your eggs in one basket.' Spread your investments across different types of companies and save yourself against the risk of non-performance of a particular company or sector. For example, the steel sector might perform very well in an economic cycle, but it might perform very badly in another one. If you invest your entire money in steel stocks alone, you will be prone to volatility, but if you invest in diversified mutual funds, it will save you from the non-performance of a particular sector or company.

Research: Doing good research is the most important thing that a mutual fund has to do. It invests its funds on the basis of research done by several analysts from various sectors in the industry. As an investor, it is very difficult for you to do research because good research needs an understanding of various aspects of the industry and the art of investing. By investing through mutual funds, an investor gets the advantage of professional research for their investments.

Costs of investment: As we know, there are various costs associated with investing in mutual funds. The fund manager will always charge a particular amount even if you are making losses on your investment. But the good part is that these charges are largely regulated by SEBI and there is a limit on the charges levied on various types of funds. This makes mutual funds a cost-efficient investment tool, compared to other tools where the cost of fund management might be a bit higher.

Portfolio Churning: The markets may not always perform right. We can't just invest in a single stock and sit on it. There are risks of non-performance from particular stocks. Even if we invest in a particular group of stocks, there is no assurance that the group will keep generating good returns for you. To avoid this problem, you need to regularly churn your portfolio and keep looking for stocks which can provide better returns than your earlier holdings.

Mutual funds do this on a regular basis; their research team keeps updating them about which stocks are expected to perform better in the coming days and which ones are to be sold from the existing portfolio.

SIP is a magical tool: The best part about mutual funds is that you don't need to gather large capital to begin your investment journey. You may start with as little as Rs 500 per month, which is within the reach of anyone nowadays. The good thing is that a long-term SIP allows one to buy stocks at every level and helps investors to create long-term growth capital.

While investing through SIP, the investor must enhance the amount of SIP as your income rises. For example, if your earning has risen by 15 per cent in a particular year, you should enhance the SIP investment also by at least 10–12 per cent.

Liquidity: Why mutual funds are treated as a perfect substitute for equity is because they have liquidity as good as that of equity or debt instruments. You can buy or sell as per your wish; nowadays you can get the redeemed amount within forty-eight hours directly in your bank account. The only mutual funds which do not have instant liquidity are ELSS (Equity Linked Saving Schemes) which lock in your investments for at least three years, and you will not be able to withdraw before the completion of the lock-in period.

How to Select a Debt Fund

Selection of mutual funds is a critical issue; our first thought while thinking about selecting a mutual fund is the returns it has generated. But this is largely true for equity funds only. We must remember that equity is not the only tool of investment in the markets and that debt is equally important to balance the portfolio. While selecting a debt mutual fund to invest in, we need to consider a lot of factors other than returns. In the upcoming section, we will discuss some of those factors:

Safety, not Past Returns: This is the very basic reason why we invest in a particular debt mutual fund. If there is any element which affects the safety of your debt fund, you must completely avoid it. Various investors just have a look at the past returns of the fund and then decide to invest in it, but for debt funds, it is not a good approach. We must pay attention to the safety of the invested capital first.

To do this, we must closely examine the portfolio of that particular mutual fund. Anything suspicious about the companies to which it has lent makes it prone to default. We need to see if it has lent any money to any company which is facing financial trouble or is at default of risk. If yes, this fund is to be avoided completely.

For example, in today's scenario, if any mutual fund has lent a huge amount of money to any gaming company today, I would avoid it. This is an industry which has been facing an existential crisis since the implementation of GST on gross value. We need to understand that to pay back the money borrowed, the company's business model must be sustainable and that is a factor which affects the safety of a debt mutual fund.

Liquidity: Another very important point while selecting a debt mutual fund is to check the liquidity of the fund. This is why I don't find FMPs very suitable because they come with a particular lock-in period and restrictions of withdrawal. I must be able to withdraw my investment whenever I need it. Even if I have to pay certain exit charges, I should be able to withdraw it because I might face an emergency at some point. To ensure this, I need to keep tracking the AUM of my invested mutual fund which ensures that my money is easily withdrawable. If there is any large withdrawal in recent times, it is time to worry.

Returns: As we have discussed, while we must always regard the safety and liquidity of our stocks above the returns, we must also be mindful of the returns. Two important considerations are the Yield to Maturity and the duration for which your money is lent to the borrower by the mutual fund. In case the money has been lent for a very long period, it is best to avoid that fund. Just as in the case of equity funds, past returns are not the perfect parameter. We need to understand both the above factors to check for the average returns of the debt fund.

Finally, we need to understand that just like equity, debt funds too have the power to eliminate your capital. The money which we lend to a mutual fund is again lent to some corporates; any default by those corporates can eliminate our capital completely. To save ourselves from this situation, we should always consider safety as the most important factor for debt mutual funds.

Five Pointers to Keep In Mind for Equity Funds

Equity mutual funds are one of the best investment tools available in the markets. This is especially so for those investors who don't have enough knowledge and time to track and trace their funds. Still, we need to put a lot of effort into selecting the right funds to invest in. If you want to drive your vehicle at 100 km per hour, you need to look for a suitable road. A bad decision can end up in a crash. The same is the case with mutual funds. Before investing, we need to look for some factors. Here are five of the most important ones:

Fund Size: This is probably the most important factor to be considered before investing in equity mutual funds. AUM is the amount of money which is managed by a particular mutual fund. Before investing, we should examine the AUM of that fund. For example, if the AUM of any fund is as low as Rs 500 to Rs 1000 crore, the investors of these funds may face liquidity issues. So when you want to sell your investments, the fund will have very little liquidity to pay you back. In case the markets go through bad times and there is greater redemption pressure, the fund house will have to sell more and more, leading to NAV deterioration.

On the other hand, if the fund has a very large AUM, it will always face the problem of investment avenues. Sometimes we see that funds with very large AUM have to keep unnecessary cash with them because they cannot find suitable investment avenues, impacting the returns for investors. We need to look for those funds which have an average size of AUM like Rs 3000 to Rs 5000 crore.

Turnover ratio: A turnover ratio is used to reflect the amount of a mutual fund's portfolio that has changed within a given year. It reflects how many times the mutual fund has been changing its portfolio. There are a few funds which are very active and keep changing their portfolio every month; this is not beneficial to us because we are looking at it as an instrument for long-term investment. On the other hand, there are funds which are lethargic and don't reshuffle or churn the portfolio even during bad times, causing them to lose good opportunities.

A mutual fund must act as per the market scenario and keep looking for good opportunities for investment.

Manager Track Record: While investing in a particular mutual fund, we always see the returns from a short term to a very long term. What we need to focus on is the fund manager under whose leadership those returns were generated. Often the fund managers for particular mutual funds are changed. This affects future returns on either side. To avoid this, we must study the fund manager. Only index funds are meant to perform automatically; if we wish to earn better returns from active equity funds, we need to see who is handling our money.

Beta: Beta is an important factor which traders and investors look for before investing in equities. It is just as important for mutual funds. An equity mutual fund is nothing but a consolidated equity portfolio. If the beta of a mutual fund is more than one, it has the power to generate better returns than the market, but during bad times, it could underperform. On the other hand, a beta of less than one will cause the markets to underperform while going up but it will be comparatively safe when the market falls.

When we look at beta, there is no standard method of selecting an equity mutual fund. Instead, we should look at our own risk profiles. If you are an aggressive investor, you can go in for a higher beta fund, and in the case of a defensive approach, a lower beta will help you.

Standard Deviation: Standard deviation of mutual funds return is a purely statistical tool. It tells us how far a particular fund's returns might deviate from what it has been giving historically. So, for example, if a particular fund has been generating 20 per cent returns per annum and has a standard deviation of seven, then in the future, it can either provide 27 per cent or 13 per cent returns. Which means that the number of standard deviations is the margin of performance on either side for an equity mutual fund. Technically, it signifies the volatility of a particular fund.

Mistakes Made in Mutual Funds

If selected wisely, mutual funds can be a perfect tool for wealth creation for any investor. Unfortunately, investors opt for the wrong funds, which give them average returns. To eliminate these issues, we must avoid making various mistakes which investors make while selecting a mutual fund. Some of these mistakes are as follows:

Lock-in Funds: The most important feature of equity is liquidity; by choosing a lock-in fund, we also lock in our liquidity. Another big problem with lock funds is that sometimes we have to bear the continuous underperformance of a fund and we cannot withdraw from the fund, even if we want to. On the other hand, funds with lock-in periods give the fund manager the liberty to have funds for a longer term and to select stocks which might perform in the future. At the same time, since some of the stocks are underperforming, the fund does not face redemption pressure.

Buying an NFO: This particular point is directly related to investor awareness in India. Many investors still think that an NFO is like an IPO and comes with cheaper valuations. This is false. An NFO brought in by a fund is as good as a fund bought after ten years of the NFO; it is neither cheap nor expensive because it does not have any intrinsic value. Rather, it derives its value from the stocks it holds.

ULIPs are ULIPs, not mutual funds: A lot of investors invest in ULIPs because they consider them as good as mutual funds. While the investment style is similar to mutual funds, the administration and regulations are completely different. The structure of the charges in ULIPs are comparatively higher and more extensive than those in mutual funds.

Here, we need to understand that the basic objective of the ULIP is to provide insurance cover; investment is the secondary objective. In the case of mutual funds, the primary objective is investment which makes a lot of difference in the overall approach.

Buying Sectoral Funds: Sometimes investors are lured to sectoral funds because they believe that a particular factor will perform better in the future. This could be true but sectoral funds can also be very risky. To invest properly in sectoral funds, we need to understand our own risk profile. You need to be a high-risk-taking investor with excess capital to do the same. A moderate risk-taking investor must avoid investing in sectoral funds. There are many instances where we have seen sectoral funds grossly underperforming the market for an extended period of time.

Mutual Funds Markets in India: Important Aspects

The mutual fund market in India has experienced significant growth over the years. This investment tool, accessible to a few in earlier years, has now reached almost every home. In recent times, the value of the mutual fund portfolio has reached Rs 15 crore and is still growing. While understanding various types of mutual funds, we need to understand various aspects associated with it.

Regulation and Oversight: The mutual fund industry in India is regulated by SEBI, which lays down the regulatory framework and guidelines for mutual fund operations. In the past few years, the decisions taken by SEBI have largely been in favour of the common investor. One of the most important decisions taken by SEBI was to do away with the entry load and allow investments through the direct mode; this has saved a huge amount for investors. Another important decision was related to 'skin in the game' where the fund managers must invest a certain amount of their own salary in the scheme which they are managing.

Systematic Investment Plans (SIPs): SIPs have gained immense popularity in India. They allow investors to invest a fixed amount regularly (monthly or quarterly) in a chosen mutual fund. The minimum amount that we can invest in a mutual fund is Rs 500. The best part of SIP is that it encourages a disciplined investment approach in investors. As of now, we have around seven crore live SIP accounts with over Rs 10,000 crore flowing into SIPs per month in India.

Distribution Channels: Mutual funds in India are distributed through various channels, including Asset Management Companies (AMCs), banks, financial advisers, online platforms and direct plans offered by AMCs. There are around 1300 registered mutual funds advisers, of which more than 65 per cent are individual licence holders. It is quite evident with the growth of inflows in mutual funds that the nation needs many more mutual funds advisers.

Expense Ratios: An expense ratio is the amount which the mutual funds management company, technically called the asset management company, charges as a professional fee. The total expense ratio (TER) includes expenses like sales and marketing, advertising expenses, administrative expenses, transaction costs, investment management fees, registrar fees, custodian fees, audit fees—as a percentage of the fund's daily net assets. SEBI has mandated a transparent fee structure, known as the expense ratio, for mutual funds. This ratio represents the annual costs associated with managing a mutual fund, relative to its assets. Low-cost options, such as index funds and ETFs, have gained traction.

Effective from 1 April 2020, the TER limit has been revised as follows:

Assets Under Management (AUM)	Maximum TER as a Percentage of Daily Net Assets	
	TER for Equity funds	TER for Debt funds
On the first Rs 500 crore	2.25 per cent	2.00 per cent
On the next Rs 250 crore	2.00 per cent	1.75 per cent
On the next Rs 1250 crore	1.75 per cent	1.50 per cent
On the next Rs 3000 crore	1.60 per cent	1.35 per cent
On the next Rs 5000 crore	1.50 per cent	1.25 per cent
On the next Rs 40,000 crore	Total expense ratio reduction of 0.05 per cent for every increase of Rs 5000 crore of daily net assets or part thereof	Total expense ratio reduction of 0.05 per cent for every increase of Rs 5000 crore of daily net assets or part thereof
Above Rs 50,000 crore	1.05 per cent	0.80 per cent

In addition, mutual funds have been allowed to charge up to 30 bps more, if the new inflows from retail investors from beyond the top 30 cities (B30) cities are at least (a) 30 per cent of gross new inflows in the scheme or (b) 15 per cent of the average assets under management (year to date) of the scheme, whichever is higher. This is essentially to encourage inflows into mutual funds from Tier Two and Tier Three cities.

Investor Education: Awareness and investor education initiatives have played a crucial role in enhancing mutual fund participation. AMCs, the regulatory authorities and the exchanges regularly conduct awareness campaigns to educate investors about the benefits and risks of mutual fund investments. In these seminars or meetings, mutual fund experts elaborate on various aspects of mutual funds and how an investor can build a long-term portfolio with regular investment. As per the available data in FY2022–23, NSE conducted 5000 investor awareness camps.

Digital Transformation: The entire digital continuum has changed the way India has been investing over the years. Online platforms and mobile apps have made it easier for investors to research, invest and manage their mutual fund portfolios. Investors can invest in mutual funds not just through mutual fund companies' platforms but also through brokers, registrar and exchanges' platforms. Nowadays, most financial and non-financial transactions are happening through the online mode.

The mutual fund market in India continues to evolve, offering investors a range of investment options to achieve their financial goals. Over the years, digitization has helped the Indian mutual funds industry. Unfortunately, the Indian mutual funds industry still lacks investor awareness. A large part of the population is still not using this as their preferred investment tool just because they are not aware of its overall functioning.

The efforts of SEBI and other agencies in organizing investor awareness programmes has helped raise the numbers.

Other Investment Vehicles in India

Just like global financial markets, Indian markets offer a diverse range of investment vehicles that cater to various risk profiles, financial goals and investment horizons. Beyond equity shares and mutual funds, there are several investment tools which can help the investor create long-term wealth as per individual goals. Here are some prominent investment options available in India:

Fixed Deposits (FDs): This is probably the oldest method of savings used by Indian investors. Banks and financial institutions offer fixed-term deposits that provide a fixed interest rate over a specific period, ensuring capital protection. For those who are very conservative in their approach, fixed deposits are always a safe mode of investment. From the perspective of the bank or financial institution, it works as a very affordable fund-raising instrument. Since it is medium to long term in nature, it provides stability to treasury operations too. The data released by RBI shows that time deposits (includes FDs) with banks stood at Rs 164 lakh crore as of 13 January 2023. This is an increase of 8 per cent over Rs 151.9 lakh crore as of 31 March 2022.

Public Provident Fund (PPF): A long-term savings scheme with tax benefits, PPF offers attractive interest rates and is backed by the government. It is designed to encourage regular savings and financial security for individuals. It remains one of the most popular debt-based saving instruments. With a fixed maturity period of fifteen years, it makes PPF ideal for long-term goals like retirement planning or children's education.

National Pension System (NPS): NPS is a retirement savings scheme that allows individuals to contribute systematically during their working years and receive a pension in their retirement. The scheme was introduced in 2004 and was made mandatory for all the new recruits of government organizations. For private companies, it is optional. However, unlike other investment tools, withdrawals from this scheme are permitted only at retirement or under some exceptional circumstances. In August 2023, the total AUM of NPS had crossed Rs 10 lakh crore, which was a great milestone for the scheme. The scheme is managed by PFRDA, which works as a regulator.

Sovereign Gold Bonds (SGBs): SGBs are government securities denominated in grams of gold, providing an alternative to physical gold investment. SGBs are a financial instrument offered by the Government of India to enable individuals to invest in gold in a more structured and secure manner. The best part of this scheme, introduced in 2015, is that the investor does not have to hold gold physically; he can invest in gold by just holding it virtually. With the advantage of the price movement, the investor additionally gets 2.5 per cent interest per annum.

Real Estate: With the growth of the Indian economy in the past two decades, the demand for real estate has been phenomenal. This has made real estate a great investment tool for both direct appreciation and rental purposes. Cities like Bengaluru, Hyderabad, Mumbai and NCR region have seen a huge demand spike that has made real estate a fantastic option for investment. Although it is very lucrative, there is a disadvantage; to invest in real estate, we need to have a lot of money. This works as a huge entry barrier. Nowadays, Real Estate Investment Trusts (REITs) and Infrastructure Investment Trusts (InvITs) have also become interesting tools to invest in real estate. Although they largely work as an equity tool, they essentially hold real estate assets.

Commodities: Investing in physical commodities like gold, silver and agricultural products, or through commodity exchanges is another large volume investment tool. A lot of places in India are commodity rich and investors from those areas generally like to invest in commodities produced there. Agri commodities see a very large volume of investment. New- age exchanges like MCX and NCDEX facilitate investment in various commodities without holding those physically. One of the risk factors associated with commodities investment is volatility and the large amount of investment required. In the image below, you can see that in global F&O markets, commodity holds a large percentage.

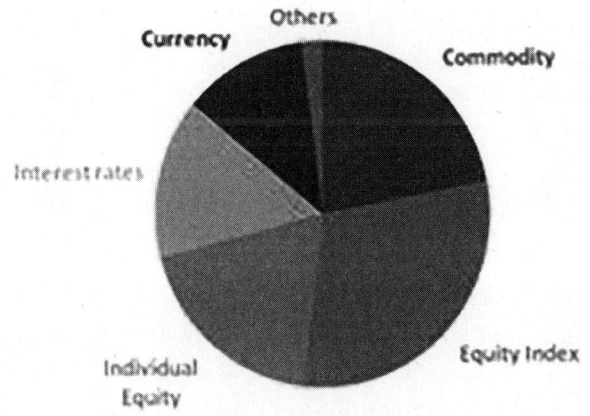

F&O Market Share

Government Savings Schemes and Small Savings Schemes: Schemes like the Senior Citizens' Savings Scheme (SCSS), Monthly Income Scheme (MIS), and Kisan Vikas Patra (KVP) offer secure and regular returns. Schemes like the Post Office Savings Account, Post Office Monthly Income Scheme (POMIS) and Post Office Time Deposit offer secure investment options. These are largely debt kind of schemes which offer safety in investment and regular payment in terms of interest accrual and payment. The money deposited in these schemes goes to the government as a loan and is utilized for national development. The rate of interest on these schemes is regularly defined by the government, keeping the market scenario in mind. As an example, we can see the rate of interest in the image below.

SMALL SAVINGS INSTRUMENT	INTEREST RATE FOR OCT-DEC	INTEREST RATE FOR JUL-SEP
Savings deposit	4.0%	4.0%
One-year time deposit	6.9%	6.9%
Two-year time deposit	7.0%	7.0%
Three-year time deposit	7.0%	7.0%
Five-year time deposit	7.5%	7.5%
Five-year recurring deposit	6.7%	6.5%
Senior Citizen Savings Scheme	8.2%	8.2%
Monthly Income Account	7.4%	7.4%
National Savings Certificate	7.7%	7.7%
Public Provident Fund Scheme	7.1%	7.1%
Kisan Vikas Patra	7.5% (115 months)	7.5% (115 months)
Sukanya Samriddhi Account Scheme	8.0%	8.0%

Alternative Investments: These include hedge funds, private equity funds and venture capital funds that offer exposure to non-traditional assets. Generally, these tools are used by large and HNI investors as the minimum threshold of investment is quite high and there is very little flexibility in the investment amount. As these invest in non-traditional tools, the risk–return ratio is also quite high.

Cryptocurrencies: This is probably one of the most money showering as well as most controversial tool of investment to have emerged in recent times. Digital or virtual currencies like Bitcoin, Ethereum, etc. are traded on various cryptocurrency exchanges in which an investor can invest. While investing in

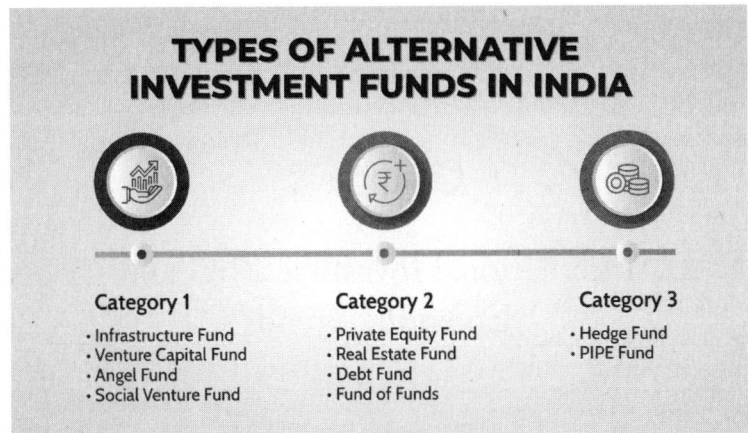

AIF

such tools, the investor must always understand that cryptos are ultra-risky and that one can even lose the principal amount. Globally, no government has accepted cryptos as legal tender. There are many financial and non-financial regulations that aim to curb activities under crypto.

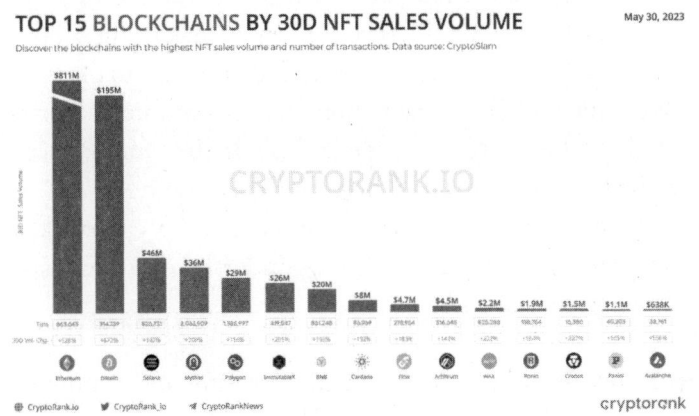

Crypto

Chapter 8

International Investing, ESG and Emerging Trends

Overview of International Investing in the Indian Stock Market

Investing in the Indian stock market can provide international investors opportunities to diversify their portfolios and participate in the growth potential of the Indian economy. For many years, Indian stock markets have been the favourite investment spot for international investors. The pace at which the Indian economy has grown in the last few years has been phenomenal. In the following chart, you can see that since 2007, Indian stock markets have seen net inflow of Rs 9.8 lakh crore in terms of foreign portfolio investments. The story does not end there. In the coming years, we are going to see even stronger flows in Indian equity.

Foreign investment in any country is not a cakewalk; you need to jump through hoops. Let us understand various aspects of FIIs investing in India.

Regulatory Framework: Regulation is the most important part of any foreign investment. FII investing is not as easy as opening a demat account for investing. To invest in India, FIIs have to take many approvals. SEBI, the regulatory authority

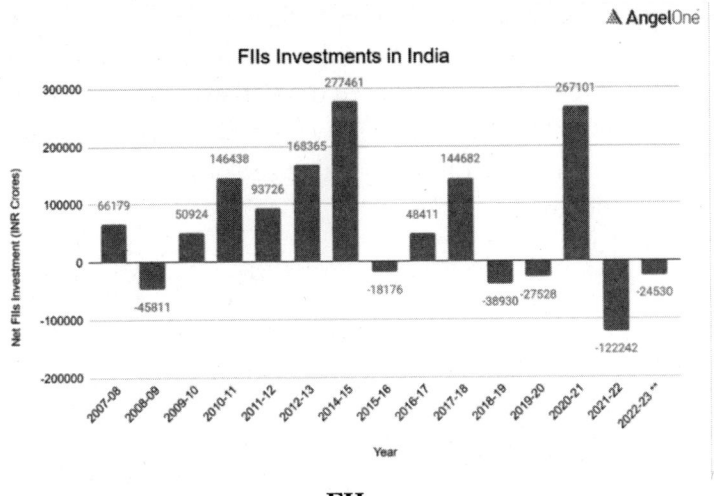

FII

that oversees the Indian securities market, has implemented various regulations and measures to ensure transparency, protect investor interests and promote the integrity of the market. Any FIIs which are not registered with SEBI cannot invest in Indian equities. Currently, India has more than 11,200 registered portfolio investors who are eligible to invest in Indian equities.

Due to the nature of the regulatory environment, foreign investors can invest via the following tools in Indian stock markets:

- **Foreign Portfolio Investors (FPIs):** FPIs are entities, including FIIs, that invest in Indian securities. They are governed by the FPI regulations issued by SEBI. FPIs are institutional investors, such as mutual funds, pension funds and hedge funds, registered with SEBI. They can invest in Indian stocks and other securities as per the regulations. FIIs are nothing but portfolio investors buying or selling in Indian equities. In the following chart, we can see that 26 per cent of the total FPI equity inflow in India over the last thirty years came in 2020–21. This validates the current state of the Indian economy which is stronger than ever. The year 2020, which slowed down the world on account of COVID-19, proved to be a boon for the Indian economy and attracted Rs 2.74 lakh crore of FPI investments in Indian equities.

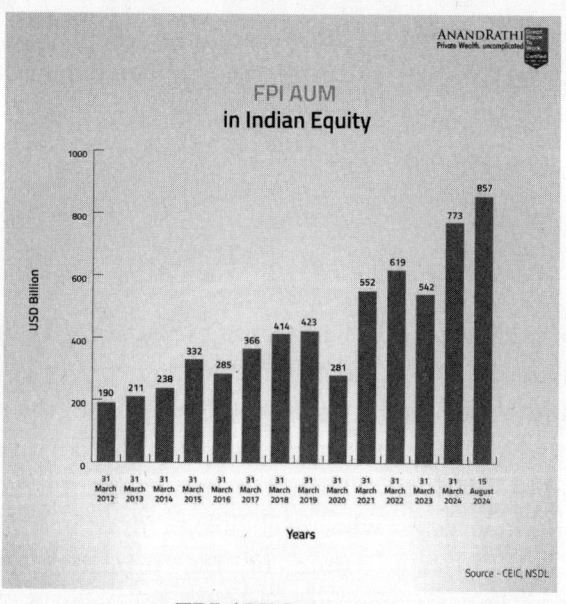

FPI AUM

- **Depository Receipts (DRs):** Another important avenue for Indian companies to raise money from the international market is Depository Receipts, which are financial instruments, issued by Indian companies, that represent underlying shares. These can be in the form of Global Depository Receipts (GDRs) or American Depository Receipts (ADRs) and allow international investors to indirectly invest in Indian stocks.

GDRs or ADRs are negotiable certificates that represent ownership of a specified number of shares of a company issued by depository banks. They can be traded and listed independently from the underlying shares. Foreign companies can trade in the stock market of any country, except the US, through GDRs. For US markets, ADRs are issued. Those holding GDRs and ADRs can surrender them to the bank and convert them into shares. GDRs are listed on non-US stock exchanges like the Luxembourg or London Stock Exchange. The GDR market is institutional and thus offers low liquidity but allows trading across many significant countries. The following comparison can explain the basic difference between ADRs and GDRs:

ADR VS. GDR

Concept

- A bank issues a depository receipt which is a transferable instrument representing the foreign companies' publicly traded securities.
- The two most common types of DRs are the American Depository Receipt (ADR) and Global Depository Receipts (GDR) which provide the investors, traders, and companies with more investment opportunities.

Basis	ADR	GDR
Listing	Gets listed on US National Stock Exchanges like the American Stock Exchange, New York Stock Exchange, or NASDAQ	It is listed on European Stock Exchanges like London Stock Exchange or Luxembourg Stock Exchange.
Issuance authority	The US banks issue ADRs which can trade in US markets	Any international bank otherwise of its home country
Compliance	All issuance has to comply with the U.S. Securities Laws along with the rules and regulations of stock exchanges	The issuer has to comply with the laws and regulations of both the home country as well as of the foreign markets
Market	Retail investor market having large participation from investors	The market involved is an institutional market.
Types	• Sponsored ADRs • Un-Sponsored ADRs	• Rule 144A GDRs • Regulation S GDRs
Disclosure Requirements	The disclosure requirement are as per Securities Exchange Commission, US	Requirements as per SEC are more stringent and onerous as compared to the GDRs.

ADR vs GDR

Name	Las
Infosys ADR	15.
ICICI Bank ADR	23.
Wipro ADR	4.9
HDFC Bank ADR	65.
MakeMyTrip	27.
WNS Holdings	78.
Lytus Technologies Holdings Ptv	0.
Dr. Reddy's Labs ADR	56.
Azure Power Global	2.
Yatra Online	2.1
Sify	1.4
Rediff.com India	0.00
Axis Bank ADR	

GDR Prices

Updated On Nov 07, 2022 Day Eno

Company	Close (USD)
State Bank of India	75.10
Axis Bank Ltd.	55.00
Larsen & Toubro Ltd.	24.75
Reliance Industries Ltd.	63.55
GAIL (India) Ltd.	6.60
Mahindra & Mahindra Ltd.	16.65

-   **Mutual Funds and ETFs:** International investors can invest in Indian stocks through mutual funds and ETFs that focus on Indian equities. These funds are managed by asset management companies and offer diversification benefits. The investors can invest in the units of the mutual funds. This gives them an indirect exposure to Indian equities.

Investment Limits: Foreign flows spell good news for any nation but an excess of foreign flows is also a concern. To control this, SEBI imposes certain investment limits on international investors to regulate foreign capital inflows. The regulators work on these limits because excessive foreign flow in any kind of company or sector will allow the FIIs to control the sector or company and they might abuse their dominant position. These limits may vary, based on the type of investor, the category of stocks and overall market conditions. It's essential to be aware of these limits while planning investments.

We also need to understand that the government keeps tinkering with these limits as per the requirements of the economy and the sector. For example, when the nation faced the economic crisis in 1991, the government had to open the FDI and FII limits for a lot of sectors. Any foreign investor can invest via the automatic or approval route. In case of the automatic route, the FII can directly invest in any company without seeking any further approval. In case any sector is covered under the approval route, then the foreign institute must make an application to the appropriate authority.

Taxation and Compliance: Any earnings must be subject to the tax regime of the nation. In the case of the income earned by FIIs, they must pay taxes on every gain. Capital gains tax, dividends tax and tax treaties between India and the investor's home country are factors to be considered. Most of the time, FIIs are given some relaxation in terms of taxation so that they invest more in a particular nation. On the compliance front, the FIIs must file all the required documents to SEBI, RBI or any other designated agency. They need to keep disclosing vital information. As on June 2023, the following is the list of companies which have a higher FII holding:

Company	FII Holding	CMP
One97 Communications	71.80 per cent	Rs 705
CarTrade Tech	70 per cent	Rs 423.4
Delhivery	67.60 per cent	Rs 355.15
HDFC	66.20 per cent	Rs 2659.8
360 One Wam	64.80 per cent	Rs 419.65
Redington	60.50 per cent	Rs 179.5
Zomato	54.60 per cent	Rs 68.45
Max Healthcare	52 per cent	Rs 533.65
PB Fintech	50.40 per cent	Rs 606.5
Shriram Finance	49.80 per cent	Rs 1410.5
Axis Bank	49.10 per cent	Rs 924.4
IRB Infrastructure	48.50 per cent	Rs 28.7
Max Financial	47.70 per cent	Rs 708.9
Apollo Hospitals	47 per cent	Rs 4810.05
Kiri Industries	46.50 per cent	Rs 290.6
ICICI Bank	44.20 per cent	Rs 949.8
ITC	43.40 per cent	Rs 442.15
IndusInd Bank	42.20 per cent	Rs 1292.2
AU Small Finance Bank	39.70 per cent	Rs 779.05
Crompton Greaves	39.60 per cent	Rs 273.9
Kotak Mahindra Bank	39.40 per cent	Rs 1935.7
Piramal Pharma	39.30 per cent	Rs 81.3
Mahindra & Mahindra	39.20 per cent	Rs 1334.7
Standard Industries	38.90 per cent	Rs 26.7
Aavas Financiers	38.80 per cent	Rs 1393.7

Research and Due Diligence: FII always comes at a higher cost and anyone investing millions of dollars into any nation, sector or company will not do so without extensive research. The FIIs also conduct extensive research before investing into any company or sector. They start with the nation's economy, then research the sector and then the company. Unlike local institutions, FIIs will never hold too many shares. Instead, they would prefer to hold a few companies. For example, Mobius Capital Partners LLP, operated by world-renowned investor Mark Mobius, owns only three companies in India. Whereas local and domestic institutions hold multiple companies. The research conducted by the FIIs is also useful for retail investors as this research contains extensive information and data about the nation, sector and company in which FIIs are invested.

Emerging Trends—Fintech and ESG Investing

Technology and Stock Markets: The world of finance is getting larger day by day. The same is the case with stock markets. Today, the stock markets have entered our pockets. Trades are just a single click away. With the help of technology, buyers and sellers are getting closer, research is getting faster and more accurate. Algo is ruling the trading markets.

Most of the trading volume happens through discount brokerages, which operate in 100 per cent online mode. Technology is now the present and the future of markets. Nowadays more than 30 per cent of the overall trading volume comes from mobile apps and Algo trades make up around 60 per cent of the overall exchange trading volume. In this section, we will understand how fintechs are impacting Indian stock markets. Incidentally, nowadays even NSE and BSE are nothing but fintechs.

Online Trading Platforms: Fintech companies have developed user-friendly online trading platforms that enable individuals to trade stocks, derivatives and other financial instruments from the comfort of their homes. These platforms provide real-time market data, advanced charting tools and seamless execution of trades. The best part of these platforms is the cost-effectiveness and ease of trading. Many years ago, traders had to make a beeline for trading offices. Then came the online trading system but it was largely restricted to trading houses only. Today trading apps are ruling the markets. With state-of-the-art facilities and fantastic Internet connectivity, these trading apps are the future of trading in Indian stock markets.

Online Mutual Funds: The way Indian fintechs are growing, they are not only revolutionizing the front-end of the financial world but improving the back-end too. Now besides buying and selling mutual funds, we can do most of the non-financial transactions via the CAMS and Karvy apps. Investors do not have to head to service centres; the bulk of transactions are being done online. Besides, platforms like BSE and others are also contributing to the growth of the mutual funds industry.

Use of Technology by Regulators: In the Indian financial system, the regulators too are using technology to a great extent. Reporting, surveillance and other actions have gone online now. Regulators like MCA, RBI and SEBI have been using technology extensively. MCA 21, Online Filing and Disclosure Systems, Electronic Data Gathering, Analysis and Retrieval (EDGAR) System, Market Surveillance and Risk Management, SEBI Complaints Redress System (SCORES), Regulatory Technology (RegTech), E-IPO, etc. are examples of technological initiatives by SEBI.

The growth of fintech in the Indian stock market has created investment opportunities in companies involved in digital payments, lending platforms, wealth management and insurtech. Investors should consider factors such as market share, growth potential, regulatory environment and competitive landscape while evaluating fintech stocks in India.

ESG Investing in the Indian Stock Market

Environmental Sustainability: With growing concerns about climate change, companies in India are increasingly focusing on environmental sustainability. This includes investments in renewable energy, energy efficiency, waste management and sustainable practices. Investors interested in ESG investing look for companies committed to reducing their carbon footprint and promoting green initiatives. Investors are quite cautious about investing in those companies which are creating pollutants in the environment, specifically companies which are responsible for carbon emissions and have a huge carbon footprint. Companies like ITC, Reliance, HPCL, BPCL, etc., whose business is part of the domain that deals with carbon emissions and massive carbon footprints, are among the non-favourites of ESG-based funds. On the other hand, companies which are into electric mobility and clean energy are the favourites of ESG-based investors.

Social Responsibility: Indian companies are becoming more conscious of their social impact. They are implementing initiatives related to employee welfare, diversity and inclusion, community development and social welfare. ESG investors can consider companies with strong corporate social responsibility (CSR) programmes and positive social contributions. Earlier, companies like PepsiCo and others were criticized for harming the environment and contaminating the water and other resources. This prompted companies to reconsider their actions towards the environment and society. PepsiCo recognized the importance of water conservation and has set goals to improve water efficiency in its operations. The company aims to replenish the water it uses in its manufacturing processes, focusing on water-stressed areas around the world. Companies like ITC, predominantly in the tobacco business, has undertaken large-scale afforestation projects to combat deforestation and promote environmental sustainability.

Corporate Social Responsibility

Good Governance: Governance practices have gained prominence in the Indian stock market. Investors are placing importance on factors such as transparency, board independence, ethical standards and shareholder rights. Companies with robust corporate governance frameworks are likely to attract ESG-conscious investors. Specifically, after the debacle of large companies like Satyam Computers, the regulators have become more vigilant and disclosures have become mandatory. ESG-based investors do not like to invest in those companies which are not transparent in their conduct. Companies like Yes Bank, CG Power and IL&FS have also faced the ire of ESG investors for being non-transparent in their conduct. Factors like independent directors and having fair business practices are now of great significance in any corporate operation.

We must understand that ESG is the future of investing. As regulators and corporates become more vigilant about environment and governance, it is inevitable that companies follow the ESG path or see the exit of large investors. Overall, ESG considerations are becoming increasingly relevant in the Indian stock market, driven by regulatory changes, investor demand and the need for sustainable practices. This trend is expected to continue as stakeholders recognize the importance of balancing financial returns with environmental and social impact. In the following image, we can see the most popular ESG-based stocks in India.

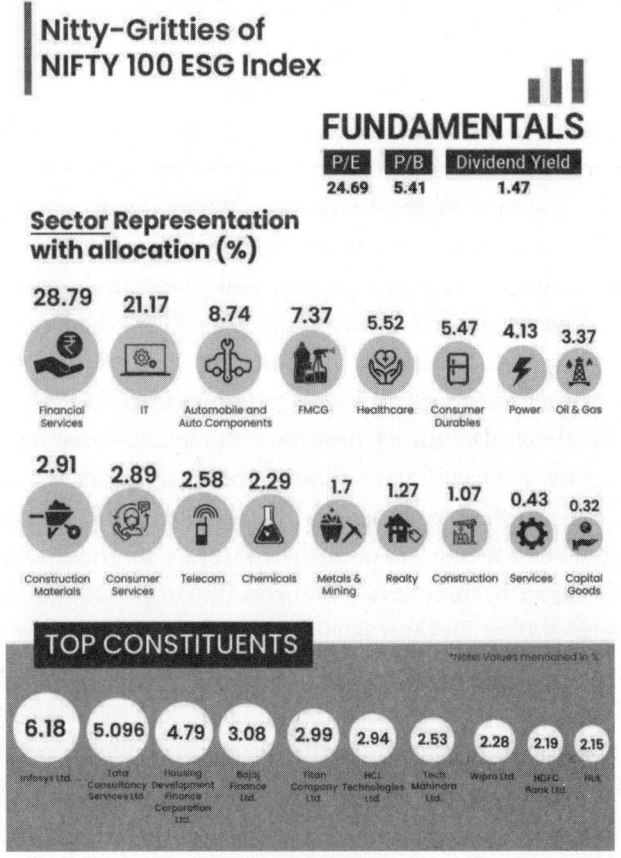

ESG Funds

Chapter 9

The Future

Future Prospects of the Indian Economy

We all know the history of Indian stock markets and we are all convinced that things can only get better.

Economic Growth: India is expected to maintain its position as one of the world's fastest-growing major economies. In 2023, the rest of the world was struggling to grow. That the Indian economy emerged strong after COVID-19 is commendable. Moderate inflation and diversified growth has been unique to the Indian economy since COVID-19 hit. The GDP growth chart shows the way the Indian economy has outperformed most of the large economies in 2023.

The chart also shows how the Indian economy has been fighting domestic inflation. Even when the entire world was battling high inflation, India was able to contain it. The past says it all. One of the reports published recently by the investment giant Morgan Stanley states that the Indian per capita income will be $5200 by 2032; it is currently $2200, amounting to an impressive 10 per cent CAGR. It also estimates that India's export market share will rise to 4.5 per cent by 2031, nearly twice the 2021 levels, with broad-based gains across goods and services exports and that there will be a major shift in the consumption basket. So many good things are waiting for India going ahead.

GDP Growth

Consumption Boom: India's rising middle class and increasing disposable incomes are driving a consumption boom. The way the Indian middle class is emerging and rising up into the upper middle class zone will boost consumption in the Indian economy. At the same time, the growing number of start-ups and upgraded salaries are driving another layer of consumption.

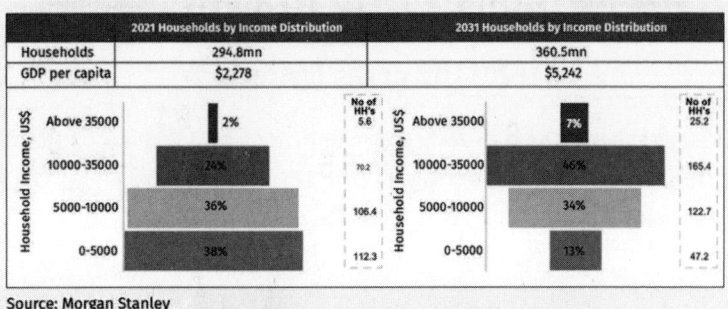

Source: Morgan Stanley

Household Income Distribution

On the above graph, we can see that by the year 2031, around 16 crore households will have an income between $10,000 and $35,000. Just imagine the boom that awaits the consumption economy in India. From household goods to cars, the Indian economy is all set to see a rising tide of increasing consumption.

Digital Transformation: A few years ago, would you ever have imagined that India would make 9.42 billion online payment transactions on a single platform like UPI? Transactions on UPI soared to their highest levels in May 2023, with a total transaction value of Rs 14.3 trillion and a volume of 9.41 billion. India is undergoing a digital transformation across various sectors, including e-commerce, fintech and digital payments. With increased Internet penetration and smartphone adoption, digital technologies are reshaping businesses and consumer behaviours. The adoption of digital infrastructure from mobile phones to banks to regulations has supported the high growth trajectory. With 80 crore broadband connections, India is set become a tech-dominated economy.

Infrastructure Development: With 1.44 lakh kms of national highways, India is showing the world that a third world economy can build world-class infrastructure too. Beyond the roads, ports, airports and other infrastructure are also growing faster. The nation is likely to add nearly eighty airports in the next four to five years. With this kind of growth in infrastructure, a growth in the economy is guaranteed. The Indian government has prioritized infrastructure development as a crucial driver of economic growth. Investments in transportation, energy, smart cities and other infrastructure projects are expected to create opportunities for construction, engineering and allied sectors. The following graph shows you how the growth of highway construction has been in the last eight to nine years. The length of highways has increased almost 1.5 times in the last nine years. This will lead to better connectivity and higher economic growth.

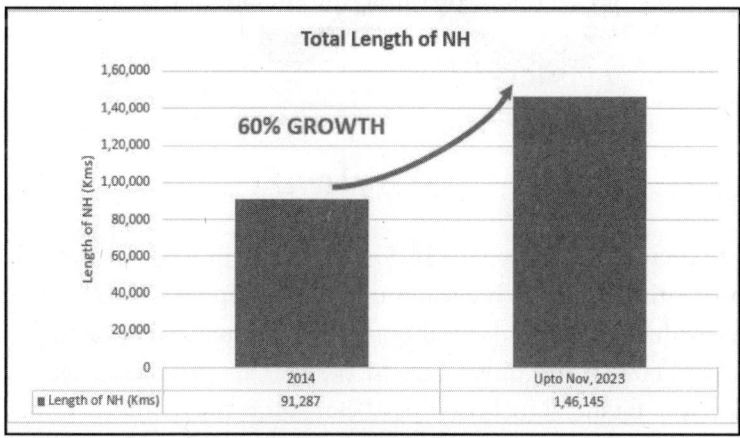

National Highways

Renewable Energy: As we have already seen, the entire world is trying to move towards sustainability and is becoming more ESG-compliant. With this move, the usage of fossil fuels as a source of energy has to reduce and the world will have to shift towards renewable energy. Sources like solar energy, wind energy and green hydrogen are the way forward. India has set ambitious targets for renewable energy generation, aiming to reduce the dependence on fossil fuels and to combat climate change. Investments in solar, wind and other clean energy sources are expected to surge. This creates opportunities for companies operating in the renewable energy sector. The current electricity mix in India is around 1:3 for fossil and renewables, and is expected to go up to 1:1 by 2030. Just imagine the kind of growth we will see in the sector.

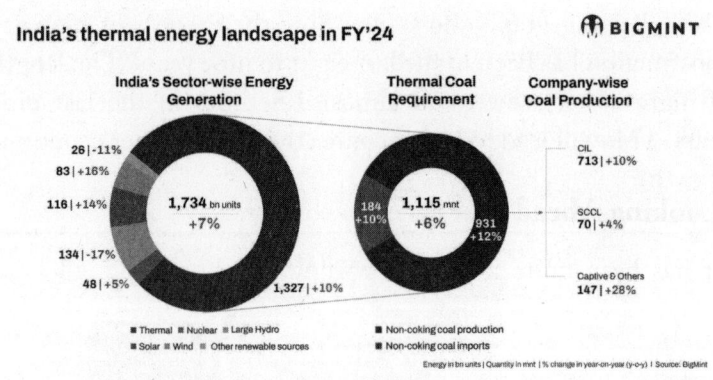

Renewable Energy

Financial Inclusion: The Indian government has been actively promoting financial inclusion initiatives, aiming to bring more individuals into the formal banking and financial system. Jan Dhan Yojana and direct benefit transfer are great examples of the way financial inclusion has been successful in India. Other moves have been expanding access to credit, digital payments and improving financial literacy. Fintech companies and digital banking platforms are well positioned to benefit from this trend. Now enhanced connectivity through faster mobile networks and banks is always accessible to the consumer. RBI has always been one step ahead in terms of providing better financial services to the end user. Facilities like NEFT and RTGS are available around the clock. While there is still a long way to go, the day even 50 per cent of the Indian population operates services like online banking, UPI and demat, imagine the kind of growth we will see in Indian financial markets.

Overall, the Indian economy is poised for a wonderful growth trajectory. Faster growth of the Indian economy will lead to better financials of companies and in turn, will lead to better performance of listed companies and superior stock returns. Going forward, the Indian economy offers prospects for growth, driven by factors such as economic development, consumption patterns, technology advancements, infrastructure investments and the government's focus on renewable energy and financial inclusion.

Looking Ahead

It has been quite a journey writing this book. We all know where to start but it is extremely difficult to end the journey. While writing the last chapter of this book, I would like to say that the global stock markets are as large as the universe. Indian stock markets are going to get bigger and will occupy a bigger portion of that universe.

At the core of Indian businesses are ethics and sound corporate governance practices, which are not seen in many parts of the world. The innovation which India is witnessing and is about to witness in the coming years is incredible. The future has lots of surprises in store for us.

By now we have understood that the Indian stock markets are a dynamic and integral component of the nation's financial landscape. They play a crucial role in economic development, capital formation and investor wealth creation. As the market undergoes continuous evolution, the implications for future research and policy changes become increasingly significant. To understand the tone of market performance, we need to understand its direction and the factors that affect it. From investor sentiments to government policies, there are thousands of factors which affect every gesture of the stock markets and here, we will try to understand a few of them.

Market Regulation and Governance: Indian regulators are quite active and have always been vigilant in terms of controlling frauds. While there have been cases like Satyam Computers which took the entire corporate governance landscape for a ride, there is still a measure of control over listed entities. The same is expected in the future from entities like SEBI, which is the regulator for capital markets in India.

The regulatory framework and governance structures governing the Indian stock markets are pivotal in ensuring fair practices, transparency and investor protection. The future efforts from regulators must be directed towards protecting investors' interests, avoiding larger scams and enhancing the standards of corporate governance for both listed and unlisted entities. Here, while discussing regulatory parts, we should consider the ease on the other side of the table. Too many regulations will kill the capital market and deter the very spirit of capitalism. It is important to check the regulatory framework before the company gets listed on any of the markets. Today, when global corporate giants have options to get listed in many markets around the globe, companies can choose those markets which have a robust regulatory framework.

There was a time when many multinational companies got delisted from India due to rising regulations and disclosure norms. The regulators need to understand and create a balance between the required regulations and disclosure norms and giving the company space to breathe.

Technological Innovations and Disruptions: Nowadays no business can grow without technology. The same is the case with capital markets where the need for technology is ever-growing. From IPOs to continuous exchange-related activities, technology is everywhere. The stock exchanges are now nothing but fintechs providing tech support to the capital markets.

From algo trading to blockchain applications, understanding the implications of technological innovations is crucial. Policymakers should be prepared to enact policies that embrace innovation while safeguarding market integrity and mitigating potential risks associated with technological disruptions. The future of stock markets will largely depend on how well the technology is implemented for traders and other stakeholders. As a market, India has done well in terms of tech implementation. It now takes just five minutes to open a demat account and now T+3 listing and T+1 settlement is a reality. Soon we might cut down this time further.

Financial Inclusion and Investor Education: A population of 140 crore with at least fifty crore working people and just ten crore demat accounts! Indian capital markets have room to grow. Another important part to be discussed in financial inclusion is the participation of women in direct equities.

Achieving financial inclusion and improving investor education are imperative for fostering a vibrant and inclusive stock market. Future research should explore strategies to make financial products more accessible to a wider population. Without educating people about the financial markets, we can't expect them to start investing. This education has to start at the school level where children can become financially literate at an early age.

Global Integration: Indian markets are going to hold a dominating place in the global economy, and it is necessary to have global integration for this to materialize. In an era of increasing global interconnectedness, research should investigate the influence of global economic indicators on the Indian stock market.

The government and regulators need to develop strategies which are pro-globalization and attract global money and knowledge. The required initiative has been taken by the government in terms of establishing GIFT city in Gandhinagar; it is now ready to become a global financial centre. In the same way, some of the important regulatory measures must also be taken. One important aspect is about the timing of the stock markets.

In this direction, SEBI has already started working and in-principle approval has already been given to let the exchange extend the derivative trading timing. Exchanges like BSE and NSE have already decided to extend the derivative trading timing in a phased manner. This will address the time lag between global and Indian markets.

Appendix

Case Studies and Applications

History of Stock Markets in India: Major Events and Learnings from Them

Stock trading in India goes back to the eighteenth century when the East India Company began trading in loan securities. Later in the 1830s, stock exchanges in India came into existence when twenty-two stockbrokers began trading opposite the Town Hall of Bombay under a banyan tree. Since then, Indian stock markets have sailed through a journey of more than 193 years. From nothing to a market cap of more than Rs 280 lakh crore. From a few companies to more than 2000 listed stocks on exchanges. The history is quite long and full of hiccups. In this section, we will try to understand some of the important events and milestones in the history of the Indian stock markets.

The First Stock Exchange—BSE

The informal group of stockbrokers organized themselves as the Native Share and Stockbrokers Association which, in 1875, was later organized as the Bombay Stock Exchange (BSE). BSE was shifted to an old building near the Town Hall. Later in 1928, the current plot of was bought and a building was constructed and occupied in 1930. In 1956, the Government of

India recognized the Bombay Stock Exchange as the first stock exchange.

National Stock Exchange

NSE was incorporated in 1992. It was recognized as a stock exchange by SEBI in April 1993 and commenced operations in 1994 with the launch of the wholesale debt market. Later, it commenced trading in the cash segment too. NSE now commands a leadership position in equity trading in India.

Securities Exchange and Board of India (SEBI)

The growing number of parties and the volume of trade created the need for a regulator for the capital markets. This led to the creation of SEBI in 1992. It was formally established on 12 April 1988 as an executive body and was given statutory powers on 30 January 1992 through the SEBI Act, 1992. SEBI is known as one of the strongest regulators of capital markets.

Harshad Mehta Days

The only positive fallout of Harshad Mehta's actions was that the common man was exposed to the magic of stock markets. Ordinary Indians began to understand how to make money from investing and trading. Harshad Mehta was most famous for his involvement in the 1992 Indian securities scam, which is often referred to as the 'Harshad Mehta scam' or the 'Big Bull scam'. He was smart enough to exploit the loopholes in the Indian banking and financial system to manipulate stock prices and drive up the stock market.

One thing which we need to understand here is that though the scam is called the 'Stock Market' scam, it was largely operated as a banking scam. Mehta illegally raised money from banks and used it inflate the prices of a few stocks. Finally, the scam was broken out in 1992 by journalist Sucheta Dalal and the markets crashed. A lot of people lost their savings and India ushered in an era of capital market regulation.

In the following chart, we can see how the Sensex and ACC, Mehta's favourite stock, reacted during the crash. The crash strengthened the requirement of Regulatory Oversight for capital markets in India. Later, SEBI was empowered by the authorities to take action on non-compliance.

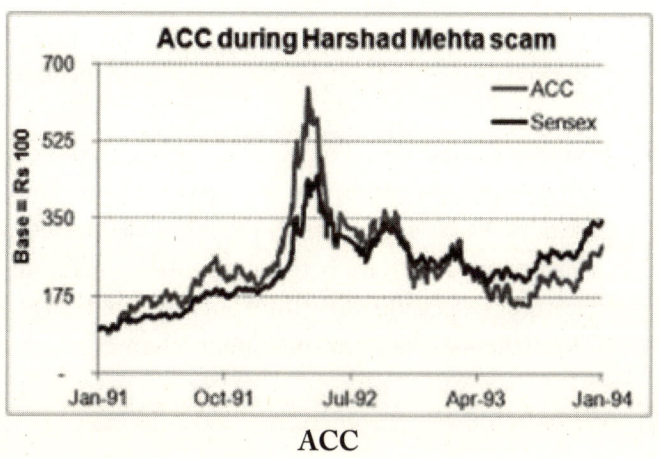

ACC

The following were the impactful learnings from this scam, which actually helped the Indian system to mature in a sense:

1. **Regulation:** The Harshad Mehta scandal highlighted the need for stronger regulatory oversight and enforcement in financial markets. It exposed the loopholes in the regulatory framework that allowed manipulation and fraud to occur.

2. **Transparency and Accountability:** Transparency in financial transactions and the accountability of market participants are essential for maintaining trust and integrity in the financial system. Investors and

regulators should have access to accurate and reliable information to make informed decisions and detect fraudulent activities.

3. **Risk Management:** The scam underscored the importance of effective risk management practices for financial institutions and investors. It revealed the risks associated with excessive leverage, speculative trading and inadequate risk assessment processes. Sound risk management practices are crucial for mitigating potential losses and safeguarding against financial crises.

4. **Investor Education:** The scandal highlighted the need for investor education and awareness about financial products, risks and market practices. Educated and informed investors are better equipped to make sound investment decisions, identify potential red flags and protect themselves from fraudulent schemes.

5. **Whistle-blower Protection:** Whistle-blowers play a vital role in uncovering wrongdoing and holding individuals and institutions accountable for their actions. The Harshad Mehta scandal brought attention to the importance of whistle-blower protection and the need to create a supportive environment for individuals to report misconduct without fear of retaliation.

The 2000s—the Stock Market Boom

The Indian stock market witnessed a period of remarkable growth during the early to mid-2000s, with the Sensex (BSE's benchmark index) reaching new highs. Due to the growing economy and population, a lot of foreign portfolio investors started entering Indian markets. These investors played a significant role in driving growth in stock markets, investing heavily in Indian equities. Several Indian companies went public, and initial public offerings (IPOs) gained popularity among investors. At the same time, the dot-com bubble hit the markets and many Internet companies went out of business.

Priceline.com was a company founded by Jay Walker, an entrepreneur with a clever solution to a real problem: every day, five lakh airline seats were going unsold. Priceline offered these seats to online customers who could name the price they were willing to pay. Consumers got cheaper flights, airlines sold excess inventory, inefficiencies were ironed out of the market, and Priceline took a cut for facilitating the process: your garden-variety win–win–win–win that only the Internet could enable. In March 1999, Priceline went public at $16 a share. On its first day of trading, the share went up to $88, before settling at $69. This gave Priceline a market capitalization of $9.8 billion, the largest first-day valuation of an Internet company to that date. A few investors were concerned that in its first few quarters in business, Priceline had racked up losses of $142.5 million. Or that it had to buy tickets on the open market—at cost—to fulfil customers lowball bids, losing, on average, $30 on every ticket it sold. Or that Priceline customers often ended up paying *more* at auction than they could have paid through a traditional travel agent. Investors were more interested in grabbing a piece of a company that was going to change the future of business. This was just one story but there hundreds of such stories, and showing losses and demanding high valuation became a trend. In October 1999, the market cap of the 199 Internet stocks tracked by Morgan Stanley's Mary Meeker was a whopping $450 billion. But the total annual sales of these companies came to only about $21 billion. And their annual profits? What profits? The collective losses totalled $6.2 billion. Over the second half of 1999, it wasn't a question of whether or not a bubble existed; it was a question of how big a bubble it was, and when it would pop. One by one, the weakest of the dot-coms began to underperform. Falling stock prices turned into stock market delistings and then became actual bankruptcies. On 14 January 2000, the Dow Jones Industrial Average peaked at 11,722.98, a level it would not return to for more than six years. The tech-heavy Nasdaq peaked on 10 March 2000, at 5048.62, a level it would not reach again until March 2015. Nasdaq lost over 75 per cent of its value in this fall.

Imagine your investments hitting rock bottom. If the trusted stocks in your portfolio get devalued by 75 per cent, how would you feel about it? Infuriated, of course! This is what happened in 2001 when stock markets across the world fell when the dot-com bubble burst. So what exactly is the dot-com bubble and what led this bubble to burst?

The dot-com bubble refers to the period in which people were thrilled about the potential of technology stocks and the amount of profit they could deliver. These stocks led the pathway to the hopes and dreams of many who aspired to become rich. Unfortunately, the expectations of these investors did not land well. Indications that the bubble would burst began showing in the year 2000 and by the end of 2001, a key measure of these stocks, the Nasdaq Composite Index, lost at least three-fourths of its value. In simple terms, you bought something for **100 bucks and its value fell to just 25 bucks**! The impact spread around the world, directly affecting the Indian economy. The Bombay Stock Exchange fell to less than half of its value between the years 2000 and 2002. A significant number of investors lost faith in tech stocks when this happened.

Tech companies ran out of business and others hastily teamed up to survive. The financial storm of the dot-com bubble burst shook the world to its core but left some important lessons for life.

If I want to show you the overvaluation and pain that happened due to this crash just look at the following chart of one of the biggest wealth creators in the history of the Indian stock market and you will understand.

If you have kept a strict 8 per cent stop-loss in your position, you would not have had to suffer the pain. It is easy to say that Rs 10,000 became Rs 800 crore in forty years in Wipro, but if you had bought it when there was madness around this stock, for the next twenty years, your returns would have been zero.

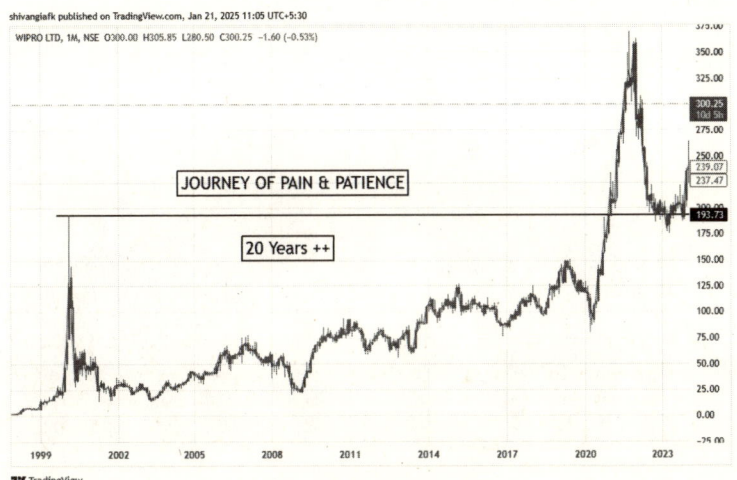

Stock Market Boom

The Great Bull Run of 2003 to 2008

The period of 2003 to 2008 was an exciting time for Indian stock markets. Almost every sector was on a roll and the markets were completely re-rated. There were many multibaggers and investors' wealth was hitting the roof. This period was characterized by a remarkable bull run in the stock markets.

Robust economic growth, driven by a burgeoning middle class and increasing foreign investments, played a pivotal role. The Indian economy benefited from structural reforms and globalization, propelling it to one of the world's fastest-growing economies. Within five years, the Sensex went from sub-3000 levels to 20,000+ and Nifty zoomed from less than 1000 to 6000+. A remarkable seven times growth for Indian markets with a staggering 45 per cent+ CAGR. This was the time when every foreign investor wanted to have a piece of the Indian growth story as the population base was also rising and India was becoming one of the largest markets in the world. In the image below, we can see how the bulls were roaring every day during the dream run of 2003 to 2008.

Growth

2008 Global Financial Crisis—The Global Dent

The global dream bull run ended in 2008 when the US sub-prime crisis unfolded, and the financial markets of the world took a nosedive. The crisis started in the US due to sub-prime lending and later due to huge defaults in mortgage payment. Sub-prime mortgages are loans given to borrowers who have bad credit and are more likely to default. During the housing boom of the 2000s, many lenders gave sub-prime mortgages to borrowers who were not qualified. In 2006, a year before the crisis started, financial institutions lent $600 billion in sub-prime mortgages, making up almost one out of four (23.4 per cent) mortgages.

Cheap credit and relaxed lending standards allowed many high-risk borrowers to purchase overpriced homes, fuelling a housing bubble. As the housing market cooled, many homeowners owed more than the worth of their homes. As the Federal Reserve Bank raised interest rates, homeowners, especially those who had adjustable-rate mortgages (ARMs) and interest-only loans, were unable to make their monthly payments. They could not refinance or sell their homes due to real estate prices falling. Between 2007 and 2010, there were nearly four million foreclosures in the US.

This had a huge impact on mortgage-backed securities (MBS) and collateralized debt obligations (CDOs)—investment products backed by the mortgages. Sub-prime mortgages were packaged by financial institutions into complicated investment products and sold to investors worldwide. By July 2008, one out of five sub-prime mortgages were delinquent with 29 per cent of ARMs seriously delinquent. Financial institutions and investors holding MBS and CDOs were left with trillions of dollars' worth of near-worthless investments.

In March 2008, Bear Stearns became the first major investment bank to collapse, sending shockwaves through the stock market. The bankruptcy of Lehman Brothers in September 2008 triggered a global financial meltdown.

In October 2008, President George W. Bush signed the Troubled Asset Relief Program (TARP) into law to buy back mortgage-backed security and inject liquidity into the system.

Banks and financial institutions globally faced a liquidity crisis, and the housing market bubble burst, leaving many homeowners with underwater mortgages. Due to the crisis and liquidity issues, central banks across the globe had to provide liquidity and interest rate support to the banking and financial system. The crisis did not stop after the banking system was affected; it affected global stock markets too. The Sensex, which had its peak before the crisis, went down to 8800 during the crisis. Even S&P, which touched a peak of 1565 in October 2007, went down to 676 during the crisis.

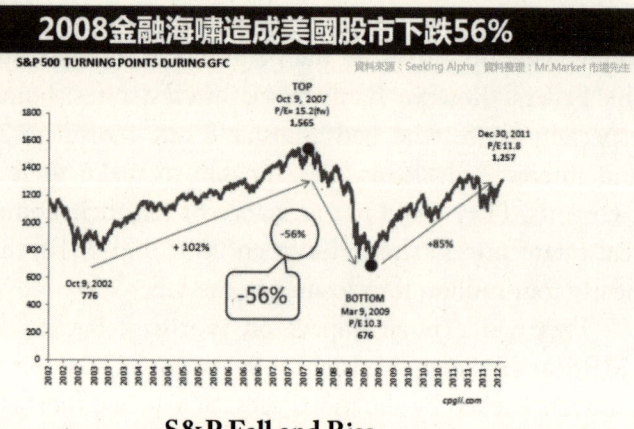

S&P Fall and Rise

From India's perspective, some of the biggest gainers and favourite stocks of retailers took more than ten years to recover from this crash. Let's understand the situation with some examples:

Reliance Returns

From every crash we can learn the same two important principles:

1. If you had a strict 8 per cent stop-loss policy and considered it as an insurance, you would have saved a majority of your capital.
2. The winners of the last season need not be the winners of the next season. In every bull run, a new set of winners emerge. Here we have taken examples of stocks which at least recovered and reached new highs. There will be hundreds of other examples of stocks which never recovered.

The COVID Crash of the 2020s—Pandemic and Recovery

The COVID-19 pandemic in 2020 led to a sharp crash in global stock markets, including India's Sensex and Nifty. The global markets started behaving unstable since the beginning of the year as COVID-19 was spreading its impact over the world. The same was the case with Indian markets which started falling from February 2020, anticipating a national lockdown, and made its bottom in the last week of March 2020, a few days after the announcement of the lockdown. This fall was a bit different from the earlier one in terms of time correction as it lasted only for a few months and the recover was even faster. On 12 March 2020, the Sensex lost more than 2900 points, its single largest absolute fall historically. The second largest fall also dates back to the COVID era.

In the right-hand side graph, we can see that the recovery after the crash was even sharper; it took most of the global markets to an all-time high. By the time various companies around the globe discovered the COVID vaccine, investor sentiments were boosted further.

SENSEX SEES BIGGEST SINGLE-DAY FALL SINCE MAY 2020

COMPANY	SENSEX CLOSING	BIGGEST FALLS (POINTS)
23-Mar-2020	25,981.24	-3,934.7
12-Mar-2020	32,778.14	-2,919.3
16-Mar-2020	31,390.07	-2,713.4
04-May-2020	31,715.35	-2,002.3
09-Mar-2020	35,634.95	-1,941.7
18-Mar-2020	28,869.51	-1,709.6
24-Aug-2015	25,741.56	-1,624.5
28-Feb-2020	38,297.29	-1,448.4
21-Jan-2008	17,605.35	-1,408.4
21-Dec-2020	**45,553.96**	**-1,406.7**
30-Mar-2020	28,440.32	-1,375.3
01-Apr-2020	28,265.31	-1,203.2
24-Sep-2020	36,553.60	-1,114.8
24-Oct-2008	8,701.07	-1,070.6
18-May-2020	30,028.98	-1,068.8
15-Oct-2020	39,728.41	-1,066.3
21-Apr-2020	30,636.71	-1,011.3

Source: AceEquity   moneycontrol

COVID Falls

Recent Developments (2021 onwards)

The most important change which has come about after the COVID crash and recovery is the enhanced participation of retail. Gradually retail participation in trading and investing activity has increased. FII selling during COVID was absorbed by the retail buyers. One more important factor is about the government's perspective about economy and business The prime minister's '*aapda me avsar*' mission has done wonders to the economy, boosting stock valuations.

On the contrary, if we talk about negative changes, then inflation and the subsequent upwards movement in interest rates have dented investor sentiment. More than India, the global inflation and chances of recession in the US economy have been a worry for the stock markets. Now India is seeing a lot of regulatory changes, and T+1 settlement and T+3 IPO listing have become a reality.

On every market fall, you will hear people say that this time it is different.

But the sad reality is that it isn't. During every bull and bear market for the last three decades, I have heard the words, 'It's different this time.' Surely, during the 1920s, the legendary stock trader Jesse Livermore heard these same words. In *How to Trade in Stocks*, Livermore said, 'All through time, people have basically acted and reacted the same way in the market as a result of: greed, fear, ignorance, and hope. Wall Street never changes, the pockets change, the stocks change, but Wall Street never changes, because human nature never changes.' Technology has advanced, regulations have improved, transparency has increased but still stocks rise and fall for the same basic reasons as they did before: people drive stock prices, and people have the same kind of emotions.

So instead of panicking at every fall, and thinking that this time it's different, let us understand how the markets have performed in the last few decades and how have they reacted and recovered post-crash. We should analyse how every time companies with the highest profitability growth were the first to lead every market rally and how old names never gained momentum. So it's time to become a good student of the stock market and let the market teach us new things every day.

Analysis of the Stock Market in the Last Forty Years in India

Over the past four decades, the Indian stock market has witnessed significant transformations, in terms of various aspects like the country's economic development, policy changes and global market dynamics. The most important change which we have witnessed in the last four decades is the domination of equity culture. Earlier, the stock market was not a preferred choice for investment or fundraising. Entrepreneurs were not interested in raising equity capital. The debt market, specifically banks, were the primary source of finance. Here, in this write-up, we will try to understand some of the major aspects of the last forty years in brief.

1. **The Equity Culture:** As discussed in the opening remarks, we can say that India as a nation has started seeing the equity culture. Earlier, the Indian economy was largely a closed economy and not as exposed to new-age products. In turn, there was lower demand and production, due to which the demand for capital was also low. The demand for capital was largely met by the banks, and no one was interested in capital markets.

   The year 1992 brought about a radical change in the Indian economy and the government came up with a foreign policy led by liberalization, privatization and globalization. Due to the change in policy, a huge amount of capital inflow came to India, which in turn pushed up demand and production. This led to an enhanced demand for capital which was not met by banks, hence raising equity was inevitable. Small corporations of that time went public, and the rest is history.

2. **Market Performance:** The performance of the Indian stock market has been characterized by some of the best bull runs, corrections and volatile phases and even certain painful bear phases. The first index, Sensex, which was started in 1986 with a value of 100 is now at more than 65,000, which is a fantastic 650 times returns. This is a staggering 19 per cent CAGR, better than any other global markets.

   On the other hand, Nifty, which was started in 1997, has produced even better results with more than 22 per cent CAGR. An amount of Rs 100 invested in Nifty in 1997 is now worth more than Rs 19,000.

3. **Technological Advancements**: Today, Indian stock exchanges are largely fintech. The adoption of technology has been a game changer for the Indian stock market. The shift from open-outcry trading to electronic trading platforms has increased efficiency and accessibility. With time, the reach of trading has intensified, touching the fingertips of every trader. India has always been the front runner in terms of IT implementation. When it came to stock trading, it followed the same approach. Some of the important achievements related to digitization are as follows:
   - Electronic Trading Platforms
   - Dematerialization of Securities
   - Mobile Trading and Apps
   - Algorithmic Trading
   - Regulatory Changes and E-Governance
   - Cybersecurity Measures

4. **Challenges Faced:** Despite the overall growth, the Indian stock market has faced challenges, including

market manipulation, corporate governance issues and regulatory concerns. Even when we have thousands of regulations, the markets are often hit by scams. Beyond scams, there are other challenges specifically in terms of technological issues. Exchanges and brokers face technical glitches, which become a pain point for traders. Some of the recent issues are premium spike in put and call options.

Though SEBI regularly keeps a track of these issues, sometimes things don't get settled immediately.

5. **Investor Participation**: The last four decades have seen a significant increase in investor participation, with a growing number of retail investors entering the market. Now we have close to 13 crore demats in India, and the number is growing. Beyond direct trading, the collective investment vehicles also have a high participation. As of now, India has over four crore individual investors. Adding ULIPs will just inflate the numbers.

Conclusion: The journey of the Indian stock market over the past forty years shows our ability to adapt as per the changing global environment. The most important change in the last forty years has been the change of equity culture. Specially after the Indian markets' re-rating during 2003 to 2007, the mindset of Indian investors has changed, and they have started believing that equity can be a better option compared to traditional ones. One more change in the sentiment is that after the COVID fall and the greater recovery thereafter, a huge number of young investors joined the bandwagon. This is also reflected in the rising volumes in derivative trading. After 2020, the volumes have almost doubled. As the trend is ever rising, we are expected to see this number rising even further.

How have small caps, midcaps and large caps performed in India between 2018–23?

Large cap = Top 100 stocks by market cap rank for any given year

Mid cap = Next 150 stocks by market cap rank

Small cap = All stocks below the top 250 ranks.

1. In 2018, there were 2720 small cap companies (i.e., ranked beyond 250). Of these, two (Adani Power and Tube Investments) moved to the Mega category by 2023, clocking five-year return CAGR of 57 per cent. Thirty-two small cap stocks moved to the Mid category by 2023, delivering a return CAGR of 32 per cent in the process.

2. Next, 2686 small cap companies stayed small cap and delivered return CAGR of 7 per cent.

3. Of the 150 mid cap companies in 2018, twenty (for example, Adani Enterprises, Varun Beverages, Adani Energy, Trent, LTIMindtree, Indian Hotels, Divi's Labs, Tata Power, Berger Paints, Torrent Pharma, Chola. Inv. & Fin.) moved to Mega by 2023, delivering an average 25 per cent return CAGR in the process. Sixty-eight mid cap companies stayed Mid (10 per cent return CAGR) and sixty-two slipped to the Mini category (-11 per cent return CAGR).

4. Finally, of the 100 Mega companies in 2018, seventy-three stayed as Mega (10 per cent return CAGR), twenty-six slipped to Mid (-8 per cent return CAGR), and one slipped to the Mini category (-40 per cent return CAGR).

- Note: During the 2018–23 period, the benchmark return was 12 per cent.

Conclusion: The most focused area for high-performing stocks is the Mid category, i.e., 150 stocks with market cap rank 101 to 250. Fifteen to twenty of these stocks (10 per cent+) will cross over to the Mega category and deliver handsome returns in the process. As a category, this is not as volatile or risky as small cap plus has huge potential. As a beginner, this can give us a consolidated list to work on.

Last Five Years' Biggest Wealth Destroyers Study

Six of the top ten wealth-destroying companies are from the financial sector (including insurance). Among these wealth destroyers, the finance segment turned out to be the third biggest.

Company	Wealth Destroyed		Price
	INR bn	% Share	CAGR (%)
Vodafone Idea	1,393	8	-34
Yes Bank	589	3	-45
IOCL	566	3	-8
Indiabulls Housing	491	3	-40
IndusInd Bank	478	3	-10
Bandhan Bank	474	3	-16
Coal India	433	3	-6
New India Assurance	422	2	-23
General Insurance	404	2	-18
Indus Towers	393	2	-16
Total of Above	**5,643**	**33**	
Total Wealth Destroyed	**17,305**	**100**	

Acknowledgements

We would like to extend our heartfelt and most sincere thanks to all in our subscriber family. You are our real motivation to spread financial literacy.

To our family and friends for being on our side. To our biggest motivator, Dadaji, Rajaram Ladha. A special mention of Savitri Ladha, Preeti Ladha, Kaanan and Srishti, the women in our family for their support.

To my friend Siddharth Jain and the whole team at Invest Aaj For Kal for being an amazing support. A special mention of Shivang and Pankhuri.

To our in-laws for being pillars of strength.

To the late Ram Kumar Kankani ji and the late Swayam Rathi ji whose blessings are always with us.

To my social media friends—Pranjal Kamra, Rishab Jain, Rachna Ranade, Pushkar Raj Thakur, Neeraj Joshi, Mukul Agarwal, Vivek Bajaj, Lakshya and Raj Shamani—who always motivate us to do better.

To Manish, Ralph and the whole Penguin family for guiding us and making the book happen.

Thank you to all the readers.

Scan QR code to access the
Penguin Random House India website